PACIFIC PALATE

PACIFIC PALATE

CUISINES OF THE SUN

ALAINA DE HAVILLAND

ILLUSTRATIONS BY MOLLY SHIELDS

ABBEVILLE PRESS PUBLISHERS   NEW YORK   LONDON   PARIS

Editor: Sarah Key
Designer and Illustrator: Molly Shields
Production Editor: Meredith Wolf Schizer
Production Manager: Lou Bilka

First edition
2 4 6 8 10 9 7 5 3 1

Library of Congress Cataloging-in-Publication Data
De Havilland, Alaina.
Pacific palate : cuisines of the sun / Alaina de Havilland.
p.   cm.
Includes index.
ISBN 0-7892-0203-4
1. Cookery, Hawaiian.   I. Title.
TX724.5.H3D4 1998
641.59969—dc21   96-29571

CONTENTS

INTRODUCTION 6

BEVERAGES 12

PUPUS 22

BRUNCH 48

SOUPS 64

SALADS 80

SALAD DRESSINGS 92

PIZZAS AND GALETTES 100

FISH AND SEAFOOD 112

POULTRY 136

VEGETABLE ENTRÉES 156

PASTA 170

SALSAS, CHUTNEYS, AND SAUCES 184

DESSERTS 200

INGREDIENTS AND SUBSTITUTIONS 226

INDEX 234

INTRODUCTION

Perhaps it is its geographical location in the center of the Pacific Ocean that has made Hawaii such fertile ground for conjuring up distinctive dishes. Throughout its history, Hawaii has attracted people not only from around the Pacific but also from around the globe. The result is a true melting pot of ethnic cultures.

The Polynesians, it is believed, settled on the islands around A.D. 500, finding a few small animals, birds, bananas, coconuts, yams, fish, and not much more. About 600 years later, a second wave of Polynesians brought with them seeds and plants (including taro), pigs, and poultry.

In 1778, Captain Cook rediscovered the islands, and Captain Vancouver explored them from 1791 to 1792. Missionaries from New England, in search of fresh souls to convert, descended upon the islands in 1820, bringing with them corn bread, chowders, and saltfish. Sandalwood was Hawaii's first important export, until the stock was depleted around 1830 and sugar became the islands' chief product.

In the 1790s the Spanish horticulturist Don Francisco de Paula Marín arrived in the islands, bringing with him oranges, figs, grapes, and pineapples. He became one of the early refiners of sugar from sugar cane after devoting several years to experimentation. Even though sugar grew wild in the islands, it had not been a big part of the diet, as the islanders preferred poi, the sticky, purplish paste made from taro and eaten at every meal in combination with fish, limu (seaweed), and bananas, among other foods. Don Marín's introduction of sugar-refining methods changed all that. An American sugar firm obtained a lease on a large piece of land, and plantation life was born. The missionaries were quick to apply their energy and initiative to the fertile land and rapidly became wealthy from sugar.

At first the Hawaiians themselves worked on the plantations, but they found the work boring and unpleasant, especially as they had lived a relatively carefree existence before big business had arrived. The labor shortage became an acute problem, and the solution was to be found in immigrant laborers. Over the next hundred years, first the Chinese, then the Japanese, Koreans, Samoans, South Sea Islanders, and Portuguese (mainly from the Azores and Madeira islands) were brought in. The final group of this wave of immigration to arrive were the Filipinos. Thus, over a short period of time, the islands became home to people with very diverse roots. In more recent times, Vietnamese and Thais have arrived.

The enormous cultural differences among these groups may help to account for the fact that certain food customs have survived strongly intact despite the development of a new food climate. One can discern two trends—one for maintaining the integrity of the traditional dishes, the other for creating blends and combinations from these distinct cultures. There surely can be no other spot on earth that has such a wealth of foods and customs to draw on.

From the Polynesians we have fish, shellfish, and limu (seaweed used as a vegetable, as well as for healing and in ceremonies). We also cook with such South Sea staples as breadfruit, papaya, guava, ti leaves, yams, and taro.

A Polynesian cooking method used throughout the islands is baking in an imu, or underground oven. A fire is built in a pit about 2 feet (60.96 cm) deep. The pit is filled with large stones and banana leaves are placed over them. Then the food is placed on top. Traditionally in Hawaii, a whole pig is placed in the oven with hot stones filling the abdominal cavity, and the rest of the food to be cooked is placed around the pig. This could include whole fish filled with fresh lime and sea salt wrapped in ti leaves, bananas, breadfruit, sweet potatoes, and shellfish. All this is covered with more leaves and grass mats and then spread with earth. Three to four hours later the pit is dug out and the food removed, done to a turn.

Traditionally the food is served to guests reclining or seated on the floor. Mats or banana leaves are spread out, and serving platters made of koa wood or monkeypod (rain tree) are filled with the carved pig. Individual bowls of poi (taro paste) served in coconut shells accompany the meal. The food is eaten with the fingers, and finger bowls are provided.

In the past, traditional dishes served at a luau included a variety of small fish (often eaten bones and all) and about forty different kinds of limu, generally as a relish. Today only about five kinds of seaweed are used. Green taro leaves are served as a vegetable. Traditional beverages were water, okolehao (an alcoholic drink distilled from ti root), and awa (a ceremonial drink distilled from the root of the pepper bush).Okolehao and awa are no longer available.

Fruits are generally baked whole, and coconut is used in a variety of ways—as a beverage, grated and cooked with chicken or taro leaves, and as a pudding combined with banana, taro, breadfruit, or sweet potato. Today a common dessert at luaus is haupia, sweetened coconut milk thickened with cornstarch or arrowroot.

The Samoans bake their food in an umu, which differs from the Hawaiian imu in that it is aboveground and sheltered by a thatched hut. Many foods are wrapped in braided leaves before cooking, and the food is always placed in the oven according to a particular order. The breadfruit and taro are placed in the center, then peeled bananas around the outside. Finally, the pig and fish wrapped in leaf packages are placed on top. This is all covered with banana and taro leaves. The Samoans prefer their food slightly underdone, so they cook the food only about an hour.

Samoans cook many foods in coconut milk. They feed the soft meat of the immature nut to babies and grate and strain the mature meat to extract the cream, which is wrapped in a banana leaf and baked to form a custard. They also mix the cream with seawater to make a dipping sauce. Like other Polynesians, they eat plenty of shellfish, fish, and seaweed.

Unlike the Hawaiians, who did not allow the women to eat with the men, Samoan men and women eat together, also seated on mats on the floor, with the women sitting behind the men. The food is served on mats of woven coconut leaves with a banana or ti leaf holding the food. The fingers of both hands are used to eat, and finger bowls are provided. Beverages are served in coconut shells.

Samoans introduced arrowroot, tapioca, sweet potatoes, and chicken into the diet of the islanders. For all Polynesians, breadfruit plays a large part in the diet. The Samoans pick it while it is still green, scrape off the skin with a seashell, and bake it by placing it directly in the embers of the umu. When ripe fruit is used it is baked in the skin, the charred rind removed, and the meat mashed with coconut cream. It is then shaped into balls and served on leaves.

Samoans traditionally ate unripened fruits such as avocados, bananas, lemons, limes, mangoes, oranges, and papayas. When the Samoans first inhabited their islands, they found them infested with small predatory animals that ate the fruit as soon as it ripened. To get to it first, the islanders found they had to eat the fruit before it was fully ripe. They acquired a taste for it, and many still eat it that way today.

The Chinese were the largest and earliest group of immigrants after the Polynesians. They brought with them a large number of beans and bean products, such as tofu and "long rice" (cellophane noodles), long, vermicellilike threads made by forcing mung-bean paste through a strainer into boiling broth. They also make a variety of sweet bean pastes, which they use as a filling for buns.

A major influence of the Chinese was their many ways of treating rice. They boiled it, steamed it, fried it, and combined it with meat, fish, and vegetables. They brewed it and drank the warm rice water with their meals and fermented it to make rice wine. They ground it into flour used to make noodles and dumplings. They steamed it to make puddings and puffed it to combine it with sesame seeds and sugar to make brittle.

The Chinese also brought with them numerous types of leafy cabbage and a huge variety of other vegetables, including leeks, onions, broccoli, cauliflower, eggplant, and water chestnuts. And they introduced methods for preserving foods by salting, pickling, and crystallizing.

The Japanese were the next immigrant group to arrive. The majority of them came from Yamaguchi and Hiroshima and brought with them rice and bean dishes similar to the Chinese as well as foods pickled and fermented in different ways. They also added mushrooms, fiddlehead ferns, scallions, watercress, and many other vegetables to the growing larder. They, too, had many different types of seaweeds and bean pastes, which they used in a variety of ways. An important addition to the diet was the introduction of soy sauce and miso, a fermented paste made from soybeans. Miso soup is an integral part of the Japanese breakfast. Fruits they added to the islands' cornucopia were tangerines, persimmons, peaches, Asian pears, plums, and walnuts. Like the Chinese, the Japanese also brought tea with them.

The Koreans were the last of the original plantation immigrant groups to come to the islands from Asia. Unlike the previous groups, they were mainly city dwellers. The Koreans brought with them a variety of raw pickled dishes, which have now entered the Hawaiian mainstream. The most famous of these is kimchee, a mixture of raw cabbage, daikon (white radish), and cucumber soaked in brine for a few hours, then rinsed and mixed with red pepper, garlic, gingerroot, onion, sugar, and salt, and aged for several days. Kimchee and its variations accompany all sorts of meals in Hawaii, as does shoyu (Japanese soy sauce) and Hawaiian chili water.

Among the first Europeans to come to Hawaii were the Portuguese, bringing with them sweet bread, sausage, and an island favorite, Portuguese bean soup—a thick, spicy, stewlike concoction of beans, vegetables, and meat. Another gift of the Portuguese is malasada.

This rich, doughy doughnut rolled in sugar after deep frying was originally served on Shrove Tuesday but is now so popular, it is eaten on every island every day of the year.

Not long after, the Filipinos arrived, bringing a number of dishes celebrating religious feast days. With their penchant for sweets, they also introduced many cakes, pastries, puddings, and confections. Fish plays an important role in the diet, and foods are often seasoned with a spicy fish paste called bagoong.

Filipinos also brought with them their skill at growing vegetables. You can tell a Filipino home in Hawaii, as the entire yard is covered in green vegetables not readily available in the market, squash and sweet potato vines, pumpkins, gourds, purslane, bitter melon, long beans, dasheen (a type of taro), turnips, and radishes.

Probably the most popular of Filipino dishes, and one that embodies the most distinctive cooking traits of the Philippines, is adobo. The meat—usually pork, but almost as often chicken—is first marinated in a mixture of vinegar, crushed garlic, bay leaves, salt, and whole black peppercorns. Soy sauce is added, and the meat is simmered in the marinade until tender. It is removed and fried and then returned to simmer in the broth until the liquid turns into a thick sauce, resulting in a richly exotic sour taste.

More recent is the enormous impact of foods from Thailand and Vietnam. Nowadays, we are equally at home eating green papaya salad as Caesar salad. Summer rolls bursting with fresh vegetables and shrimp and dipped in spicy sauces are a common appetizer, as are spring rolls, tasty deep-fried pastry-wrapped morsels packed with savory fillings, served wrapped in lettuce leaves with cellophane noodles and fresh basil and mint.

Both Vietnamese and Thai cooking include a large number of delicious curries and foods cooked in liquids or with a great deal of sauce. Many of these make use of fresh aromatic leaves to flavor the dishes—kaffir lime, opal basil, mint, lemon grass, cilantro. Soups are also popular, and from Vietnam comes the popular dish Pho, comprising lean beef and noodles in a clear broth served with side plates of condiments—basil, cilantro, red chilies, and heaps of bean sprouts—that you pile on top of the steaming soup as you eat, making a sort of soup-and-salad combo that is at the same time refreshingly crisp and comforting.

Closer to the present we find once again a Western influence—this time not from immigrants but as a result of the emergence of five-star resort hotels built on the islands throughout the 1980s. Created to attract the wealthy and sophisticated, the hotels recruited top chefs from Europe and California. These chefs, classically trained and at home with the much-touted Mediterranean cuisine, began to combine the familiar with the exotic. Thus a Mediterranean classic such as ratatouille became transformed, with ginger and sesame oil replacing rosemary and olive oil, and a completely new dish with roots firmly planted in the past was created. This way of looking at classical cuisine and transporting it to the East brought about the birth of Pacific Rim cuisine, which now stands very much on its own two feet, fully grown and ready to join other established cuisines as an equal at the table.

This book is about looking at the familiar with new eyes, adjusting the known with new tastes, integrating new and old flavors and preparation methods. It is also about lighter, healthier eating: using fresh ingredients and cutting down on the amount of fat traditionally included in some of these dishes. The recipes in this book rely heavily on vegetables, fish, seafood, and poultry rather than red meats and often call for vegetables to be cooked just enough to take off the raw edge, foods quickly stir-fried, or other methods that allow the fresh flavors to come through.

Though many of the dishes and ingredients may be unfamiliar, the techniques are simple and the recipes uncomplicated. And ingredients lists that appear daunting may consist largely of herbs and spices. Fresh herbs are always best, and spices should be stored away from heat and light and replaced when they lose their aroma.

With very little effort, you can prepare distinctive, attractive dishes that reflect the different cuisines of the peoples of the Pacific.

BEVERAGES

If ever there was a symbol of the easy life, something to lure us into a romantic stupor and transport us to exotic lands, it is the tropical drink—a concoction resembling not so much a cocktail as a candy-colored childhood fantasy. Lurking under the cover of paper umbrellas, pineapple spears, sprays of purple orchids, and virgin-white, aromatic gardenias lies a seemingly benign potion tasting like sweetly scented fresh fruit. The powerful punch of the libation surprises after just a few sips. Concoctions that would never be mixed at home are suddenly required drinking on arriving in the Pacific islands or entering a tropical-theme party. The Mai Tai (page 15), for example—a goblet filled just to the top with light and dark rum, orange liqueur, and a touch of pineapple juice floating on top—pretends sweetness and refreshment. Two of those on a hot afternoon, and you're ready to grab a surfboard and face the 30-foot (10-meter) surf in Waimea Bay.

But just as Pacific-inspired meals would be lacking without the flavors and fragrances of coconut, mango, banana, or ginger, so no Hawaiian gathering would be complete without tall drinks in bamboo mugs or glasses the size of mixing bowls displaying fantastic colors like lagoon blue, turquoise, brilliant orange, fuchsia, acid green, and banana yellow.

The spicy dishes in this book should be served with refreshing beverages, such as Pacific Plantation Tea (page 21), Pacific Sangría (page 18), and Passion Fruit Champagne Cocktail (page 17). For a party, serve a chilled Frosty Floral Fruit Lei (page 21), or offer cold beer from one of Hawaii's own select microbreweries, or, for the novelty, glasses of pineapple, lilikoi, or lehua honey wine, available at some liquor stores. You could also serve homemade nonalcoholic Ginger Bia (page 20).

Don your lei, hold aloft your tiki mug, and yell "aloha" as you sip from your brew of dreams. Let rip with your tropical fantasies as you muster up the courage after a few Guava Coladas (page 16) to grab a paddle and join the young men on the outrigger team, jumping aboard the canoe and paddling out to the swell, masterfully turning in synchronized harmony to the leader's cries. Then lift your paddle, eyes scanning the horizon, and wait—ready to catch and ride the perfect glassy wave back to shore. A land of sweetly chanting wahines, tanned hips swaying gracefully under moonlit palms, beckons you to paradise.

MAI TAI

4 ounces (120 ml) white rum
1 ounce (30 ml) freshly squeezed
    lemon juice
1 ounce (30 ml) orgeat syrup
1 ounce (30 ml) curaçao
Crushed ice
4 ounces (120 ml) dark rum
1 cup (250 ml) pineapple juice
Mint sprigs, lime wedges, pineapple
    wedges, and orchids for garnish

**No list of Pacific drinks would be complete without mai tai—
for those with a very sweet tooth and a reckless disposition.**

Yield: 4 drinks

Pour one-quarter of the white rum, lemon juice, orgeat syrup, and curaçao into each of four large glasses over crushed ice. Float the dark rum on top and the pineapple juice on top of that. Garnish and serve.

MARGARITA

Ice cubes
9 ounces (270 ml) tequila
9 ounces (270 ml) freshly squeezed
    lime juice
4½ ounces (135 ml) Triple Sec
Lime wedges
Salt

Distilled from the starchy root of the agave plant, tequila, either drunk straight with lime wedges and salt or served in a refreshing iced lime cocktail called a margarita, is one of the most popular liquors served throughout the tropics.

Yield: 4 drinks

Fill a blender with ice cubes and add the tequila, lime juice, and Triple Sec. Blend until smooth. Rub the rims of chilled glasses with lime, then dip in salt.

Divide the cocktail among 4 glasses and garnish with lime wedges.

MARGARITA ELENA

Ice cubes
9 ounces (270 ml) tequila
1 tablespoon Crystal Light® Passion
    Orange powder
1 tablespoon Crystal Light® Strawberry
    Kiwi powder
Juice of 1 lime

Here is a very light low-calorie margarita I invented when trying to come up with cocktails that would fit into a weight-loss diet.

Yield: 4 drinks

Fill a blender with ice cubes and add the tequila, fruit powders, and lime juice. Blend until smooth. Pour into chilled glasses.

GUAVA COLADA

6 ounces (180 ml) dark rum
6 ounces (180 ml) light rum
4 ounces (120 ml) sweetened cream
    of coconut
1/2 cup (120 ml) frozen guava
    concentrate or 1 1/2 cups (375 ml)
    canned guava juice
1/2 cup (120 ml) crushed ice
Shaved coconut and tropical blossoms
    for garnish

The tropical classic piña colada is slightly adjusted here with the addition of tangy guava juice. Frozen guava juice is available in many large supermarkets, and canned juice in Latin markets.

Yield: 4 drinks

Put all the ingredients except the garnishes in a blender and process until smooth. Pour into tall glasses and add the garnishes.

PASSION FRUIT CHAMPAGNE COCKTAIL

1 cup (250 ml) frozen passion fruit
    concentrate
1 cup (250 ml) cold water
1 bottle (750 ml) champagne, chilled

The flavor of passion fruit goes perfectly with champagne. This is a great punch to serve at a wedding or a festive brunch. Add a Frosty Floral Fruit Lei (page 21) to the punch bowl for a festive touch and to keep the cocktail cold.

Yield: 6 drinks

Mix the passion fruit concentrate with the water. Add to the champagne. Pour into glasses, or multiply the recipe and serve in a punch bowl.

PACIFIC SANGRÍA

½ pineapple, cut into ¼-inch
    (6-mm) slices
1 lime, cut into ¼-inch (6-mm) slices
1 lemon, cut into ¼-inch (6-mm) slices
1 mango, halved and cut into ¼-inch (6-
    mm) slices
2 small star fruit (carambolas), cut into ¼-
    inch (6-mm) slices
¼ cup (55 g) superfine sugar, or to taste
1 bottle (750 ml) champagne or sparkling
    dry white wine
¼ cup (60 ml) Triple Sec
1 cup (250 ml) freshly squeezed
    orange juice
1 liter club soda
Ice cubes

This fruity, light, and thirst-quenching Pacific variation of sangría is especially good at picnics and barbecues, or with paella. Any tropical fruit can be added as long as it is firm. Experiment with other fruit liqueurs, too.

Yield: 2½ quarts (2½ l)

Cut the pineapple slices into quarters. Combine the pineapple, lemon, orange, mango, star fruit, and sugar in a large 3-quart (3-l) pitcher. Add the champagne, Triple Sec, and orange juice, and stir to mix well. Refrigerate until thoroughly chilled, about 1 hour. Just before serving, stir in club soda to taste. Add ice cubes, and serve immediately.

hibiscus

PINEAPPLE PUNCH

2 cups (500 ml) strong brewed Earl
    Grey tea
1/2 cup (120 ml) freshly squeezed
    lemon juice
2 cups (500 ml) freshly squeezed
    orange juice
1/2 cup (120 ml) freshly squeezed
    lime juice
1 cup (200 g) sugar
20 mint leaves
4 cups (1 l) pineapple juice
4 cups (1 l) ginger ale or 4 cups (1 l)
    sparkling mineral water
Crushed ice

This nonalcoholic punch is perfect served with a light lunch or at an outdoor event.

Yield: 4 1/2 quarts (4 1/2 l)

Combine the tea, lemon juice, orange juice, lime juice, sugar, and mint in a 2-quart (2-l) container. Place in the freezer for 1 hour. Just before serving, combine it with the pineapple juice, and ginger ale or mineral water in a punch bowl. The mixture should be slightly slushy. Serve in punch cups.

GINGER LIMEADE

1 pound (450 g) gingerroot, grated
2 1/2 cups (620 ml) water
1 cup (200 g) sugar
1 cup (250 ml) freshly squeezed
    lime juice

This a refreshing pick-me-up on a hot afternoon.

Yield: 3 quarts (3 l)

Squeeze the ginger in a fine sieve to extract the juice; you should have 2 tablespoons.

    Combine 1/2 cup (120 ml) of the water with the sugar in a small saucepan set over medium-high heat, bring to a boil, and continue boiling 10 minutes, or until syrupy. Allow to cool slightly. Stir in the lime juice and ginger juice, and let cool to room temperature. Add the remaining 2 cups (500 ml) water, mix well, and refrigerate until chilled. Serve over ice.

HAWAIIAN GINGER BIA

4 quarts (4 l) water
8 ounces (230 g) gingerroot, grated
1 teaspoon cream of tartar
2 limes, thinly sliced
2 cups (400 g) Demerara or turbinado
    or raw brown sugar
1 package (7 g) active dry yeast
1/4 cup (60 ml) warm water
1 teaspoon granulated sugar

Exhilarating, refreshing, zingy ginger bia is brewed like beer but has an alcohol content of less than 1 percent. After 24 hours, it is no stronger than a glass of orange juice.

Try this recipe for a party, or make a smaller quantity and keep in your refrigerator to cool down on hot summer days. It is also a great aid for indigestion and is highly effective for travel sickness.

Yield: about 4 quarts (4 l)

Put the water, ginger, cream of tartar, lime, and raw sugar in a 6-quart (6-l) glass or enamel saucepan set over medium-high heat. When the mixture comes to a rolling boil, remove from the heat and cover with plastic wrap (cling film), leaving a small opening for steam to escape. Let cool to body temperature.

Combine the yeast, warm water, and granulated sugar in a small bowl and let sit until foamy, about 5 minutes. Add the yeast mixture to the brew, stir, and replace the plastic wrap (cling film), leaving a small opening for carbon dioxide to escape. Let stand in a warm, shady spot 24 hours. Strain into covered glass or plastic containers and refrigerate. The bia is now ready to drink, and will keep in the refrigerator up to 3 weeks.

PACIFIC PLANTATION TEA

4 quarts (4 l) brewed hibiscus tea
1 quart (1 l) pineapple juice
½ cup (120 ml) freshly squeezed
    lemon juice
Mint sprigs for garnish

This tea can be prepared up to one day in advance. Serve over ice cubes in a tall glass, or in a punch bowl with a Frosty Floral Fruit Lei (recipe follows). Hibiscus tea is available at health food stores.

Yield: 5 quarts (5 l)

Combine the tea, pineapple juice, and lemon juice in a 6-quart (6-l) container. Serve garnished with mint.

FROSTY FLORAL FRUIT LEI

Crushed ice
About 18 tropical blossoms, such as
    vanda orchids and nasturtiums
1 cup (100 g) mixed sliced fruit, such as
    star fruit (carambola), kiwi,
    strawberries, raspberries, and grapes
1 lemon, cut into ¼-inch (6-mm) slices
1 lime, cut into ¼-inch (6-mm) slices
1 small orange, cut into ¼-inch
    (6-mm) slices

This easy-to-make ice "lei" is an attractive way to keep a punch bowl cool at a party. As the ice melts, guests will be able to add pieces of the fruit to their drinks. It works especially well with iced tea, champagne cocktail, or any fruit juice or punch.

Fill a bundt or tube pan one-third with crushed ice. Place the blossoms on top and add another layer of crushed ice. Place a layer of fruit on top of this, and add more crushed ice. Place the lemon, lime, and orange slices standing upright in the ice. Fill up the pan with cold water and freeze. To use, place the pan briefly in a pan of hot water. The lei should slide out easily.

PUPUS

IF I had to choose just one way to introduce the cuisines of the Pacific I would throw a pupu party, a foolproof way of offering something for everyone. Sweet and pungent, spicy and hot, smooth and cool, pupus, the Hawaiian equivalent of appetizers, bring together a wide variety of different foods in miniature form. Use the nature of the occasion to inspire your selection. On a sunny afternoon, keep the pupus light and tropical. With early-evening cocktails, try spicy and exotic. At the beach, offer foods that are fruity and more substantial. In Hawaii a pupu party gives a grand opportunity to show off traditional foods of the many ethnic groups that occupy the islands.

Starting in the north and traveling counter-clockwise around the Pacific, Japan offers sushi platters (page 28), with jewellike shiny black nori-wrapped packages sliced to reveal a rainbow of ingredients; clear, cool green cucumber; dense, deep-emerald avocado; purple-tinged opal basil;

earthy-toned soba noodles; creamy jícama; and juicy coral-pink shrimp. Sushi selections work especially well with the combination of rice, fish, and vegetables all neatly wrapped in one package and easy to eat with the fingers.

Close to Japan lies Korea. Nowadays, throughout the islands, favorite lunch stops for the locals are the Korean barbecue takeout cafés, where one can sample short spicy ribs or pungent beef skewers.

Heading south around the rim we encounter Hong Kong. The foods the Hong Kong Chinese contributed to the pupu platter include dim sum, fragile little dough purses with delectable fillings, of which a delicious example is Fragrant Orange Pot Stickers (page 36).

From Southeast Asia we get light, flavorful Thai summer rolls, bursting with fresh mint, opal basil, kaffir lime, cilantro, crunchy bean sprouts, and peppery grated daikon. Further south are the complex flavors of Vietnam, including steaming bowls of Pho, the beef and noodle soup topped with crisp bean sprouts.

Moving west we arrive in the Philippines, where hints of Spain are found in many dishes. Polynesia, Hawaii, Guam, Samoa, the Marquesas, Tahiti, and Fiji all contribute exotic and exciting flavors to the dishes of the Pacific, mixing coconut, ginger, guava, lime, and papaya.

At every gathering a selection of fish and seafood of all sorts, shapes, sizes, colors, and flavors carries hints of sun and salt-sea spray. Try Tahitian-inspired Scallops in Lime Juice (page 39) and a less salty version of the traditional Hawaiian luau offering lomi-lomi salmon, Cherry Tomatoes Filled with Salmon (page 40).

Across the ocean we find more Spanish-inspired dishes, such as tantalizingly hot and spicy Mexican Crab Empanadas (page 27), packed with fresh sweet crab, and Coconut-Corn Fritters (page 59).

In the summer, place the buffet table under the shade of a tree, cover it with a colorful cloth, and sprinkle it with blossoms. Place on it a centerpiece of speared fresh tropical fruit, with bowls of bubbling hot white and dark chocolate, or set up small tables with trays of attractively arranged foods dotted around the garden. Outdoor pupu displays also work well at picnics in the park or at the beach, on an afternoon sail, or at the end of a short hiking trip.

To serve pupus I often layer trays with banana leaves, ti leaves, or monstera leaves. If tropical or large leaves are hard to come by, line the trays with cloth napkins in shades of deep-forest and pale green. Make posies of tropical blossoms to set off the brilliant colors of the dishes, or keep the arrangements simple, as the vibrancy of the food needs little help in attracting attention.

Part of the fun of a pupu party is that it requires little commitment. The guests get to sample bite-size foods and decide whether they like them or not without having to feel uncomfortable about not enjoying a dish that the host or hostess may have been slaving over for days.

When preparing pupus remember not to make too much of each recipe, for with too large a variety of food, the guests may be able to sample only one bite from each dish. With a smaller selection, figure out how many pieces in total you would be comfortable eating, and base your estimate on that. Remember that some dishes are usually favored far more than others. In Hawaii, for example, sushi and other raw fish dishes such as poke and sashimi, as well as anything with shrimp, are always very popular.

If the pupus are served at a cocktail party I suggest foods that are easy to eat with just a napkin. It is awkward juggling a glass in one hand, holding a plate in the other, and trying to figure out how to get the food in the mouth without a third hand.

For entertaining large groups of friends a pupu party is the ideal way to go. Serve pupus with pre-dinner drinks or at cocktail parties, afternoon weddings, picnics, gatherings around the pool, or casual get-togethers.

ti leaf

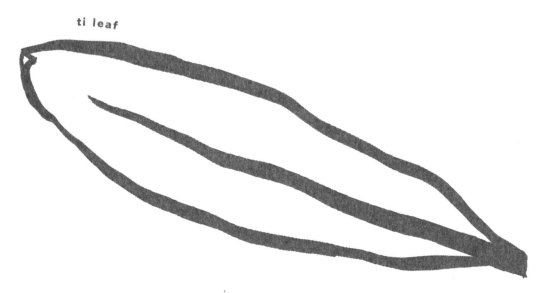

CRAB EMPANADAS

THE PASTRY

12 ounces (340 g) cream cheese, at room
  temperature
8 tablespoons (1 stick) (115 g) unsalted
  butter, at room temperature
1½ cups (215 g) all-purpose (plain) flour
½ teaspoon salt

THE FILLING

1 tablespoon unsalted butter plus more
  for buttering pan
1 medium onion, finely chopped
2 tomatoes, seeded and finely chopped
1 pound (450 g) lump crabmeat
1 tablespoon finely chopped cilantro
  (fresh coriander)
½ teaspoon cayenne
1 tablespoon mirin
1 tablespoon finely chopped basil
Salt and ground black pepper
1 egg beaten with 1 tablespoon cold water

These Mexican-inspired pastries are perfect for passing at an out-door event. Serve with chilled Tropical-Fruit Salsa (page 190) and Pacific Sangria (page 18).

Yield: 36 empanadas

Put the cream cheese and butter in a food processor, pulse a few times, then process until blended, stopping to scrape down the sides of the bowl as necessary. Add ¾ cup (170 g) of the flour and the salt, pulse until incorporated, then add the rest of the flour and process until the dough just begins to form a ball. Transfer the dough to a lightly floured surface, form it into a disc, wrap it in plastic wrap (cling film), and refrigerate at least 30 minutes.

Meanwhile, prepare the filling. Melt the butter in a large, heavy sauté pan set over medium-high heat and sauté the onion and tomato until soft, about 5 minutes. Add the crabmeat, cilantro, cayenne, mirin, and basil, season with salt and pepper, and cook 5 minutes more, stirring often. Refrigerate until chilled.

Lightly butter a baking sheet. On a lightly floured surface, roll out the dough ⅛-inch (3-mm) thick and cut out rounds with a floured 2½-inch (6.5-cm) pastry cutter. Put 2 heaping teaspoons of the filling in each round. Moisten the edges with cold water, fold in half, and press the edges together firmly with a fork.

Place the empanadas on the baking sheet and brush lightly with the egg mixture. Place the tray with the empanadas in the refrigerator to chill, and preheat the oven to 400°F (200°C). Bake about 20 minutes, or until deep gold.

PACIFIC SUSHI PLATTER

Probably the most popular pupu eaten throughout the islands, traditional sushi consists of vinegared rice accompanied by slices of raw fish, shellfish, vegetables, and garnishes rolled in nori, sheets of dried seaweed. For this Pacific Rim version of maki (sushi rolls) I've assembled a variety of colorful, interesting, and tasty ingredients that make satisfying and unusual hors d'oeuvres or an attractive lunch. Once you get the hang of it, try putting together your own combinations. It is worthwhile investing a few dollars in a bamboo sushi mat if you can find one in an Asian market or the Asian section of the supermarket. Vinegar Rice (below) and Soba Noodles (page 29) form the base for the sushi recipes. Sushi is usually accompanied by a bowl of soy sauce mixed with a little wasabi paste. Try the Sushi Dipping Sauce (page 29) as an alternative or an addition to this.

VINEGAR RICE

¼ cup (60 ml) rice vinegar
1 tablespoon mirin or dry sherry
3 tablespoons sugar
2 teaspoons salt
1 cup (4 ounces) cold cooked white or
brown medium-grain rice, rinsed

Yield: 1 cup (4 ounces)

Combine the vinegar, mirin or sherry, sugar, and salt in a small nonreactive saucepan and bring to a boil. Remove from the heat and allow to cool to room temperature.

Toss the rice with the cooled dressing. (The dressing can be made in larger quantities and stored, tightly covered, in the refrigerator up to a year.)

SOBA NOODLES

3 ounces (86 g) soba noodles

"Soba" is both the buckwheat the noodles are made from and the noodles themselves. A full-flavored, nutty-tasting noodle, it is frequently served cold with a dipping sauce and is ideal as a filling for maki. Unlike Italian pasta, which is cooked in constantly boiling water, soba is best cooked using the Japanese method called sashimi, which means "add water." This gives the noodles the right texture.

Yield: ¾ cup

Bring a large pot of water to the boil. Add the noodles, return to the boil, add 1 cup (250 ml) of cold water, and repeat when the water returns to the boil. To test, cut into a few strands: they should be firm but tender. Drain the noodles, then immediately rinse under cold water to keep them from sticking together. The noodles can be cooked and refrigerated, tightly sealed, up to a day ahead.

SUSHI DIPPING SAUCE

Juice of 1 orange
Juice of ½ lime
¼ cup (60 ml) low-sodium soy sauce
1 tablespoon Asian sesame oil
¼ teaspoon ground black pepper
1 scallion, thinly sliced

Yield: 1 cup (250 ml)

Put the orange juice, lime juice, soy sauce, oil, and pepper in a small bowl and whisk to mix. Stir in the scallion. Serve as a dipping sauce with sushi.

HOW TO ROLL SUSHI

1. Toast a sheet of nori and place it on the mat. Cook the soba and divide the noodles into three batches, lining them up lengthwise. Lay some of the arranged noodles on the nori.

2. Continue to place the soba on the nori, covering the seaweed to within an inch (2.54 cm) of the edge. Smear it with a bit of the wasabi and umeboshi pastes. Keep the layer of noodles thin so it will not be difficult to roll.

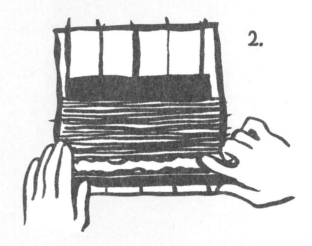

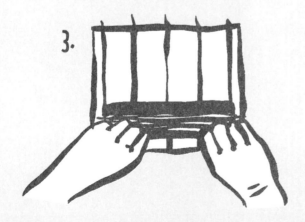

3. Firmly roll up the nori with the mat. Remove the mat, and cut the sushi roll into 1- to 1½-inch (2.54- to 3.8-cm) slices, and serve.

SHRIMP, JÍCAMA, AND CILANTRO MAKI

Yield: 18 pieces

3 sheets nori

½ cup (2 ounces) brown Vinegar Rice (page 28)

6 cooked medium shrimp (prawns), peeled and split

¼ ripe but firm avocado, thinly sliced

4-inch (10-cm) piece Japanese or hothouse cucumber, peeled, halved, seeded, and cut lengthwise into ¼-inch (6-mm) strips

12 basil leaves

12 ¼ × 3-inch (6 mm × 7.5-cm) strips jícama

3 tablespoons chopped cilantro (fresh coriander)

1½ teaspoons wasabi paste

To crisp the nori, toast sheets, shiny side down, over a flame or other direct heat. Place a sheet of nori on a bamboo sushi mat or cloth napkin with the long side toward you. Divide all the remaining ingredients in three. Spread the rice over the nori to within 1 inch (2.5 cm) of each long edge. Lay the shrimp, avocado, cucumber, basil, jícama, and cilantro in narrow rows across the middle of the rice. With your finger spread wasabi along the near edge of the nori. Carefully lift the edge of the mat closer to you and fold the nori over the filling, using a tucking and pulling motion so the sushi is firmly packed. Squeeze gently to make firmer. Unroll the mat and with a sharp, thin-bladed knife, trim off either end. Slice the roll into six pieces. Repeat with the remaining nori and filling.

jícama

SOBA AND VEGETABLE MAKI

Yield: 18 pieces

3/4 cup cold cooked soba noodles

3 tablespoons umeboshi or balsamic
vinegar

3 sheets nori

4-inch (10-cm) piece Japanese or
hothouse cucumber, peeled, halved,
seeded, and cut into 1/4 × 2-inch
(6 mm × 5-cm) strips

1/4 ripe but firm avocado, thinly sliced

6 tablespoons (45 g) grated carrot

3 tablespoons alfalfa sprouts

1 1/2 teaspoons wasabi paste

Toss the noodles in the vinegar and set aside. To crisp the nori, toast sheets, shiny side down, over a flame or other direct heat. Place a sheet of nori on a bamboo sushi mat or cloth napkin, with the long side toward you. Divide all the remaining ingredients in three. To make each maki, first place noodles on the nori, to within 1 inch (2.5 cm) of each long edge. Then lay cucumber, avocado, carrot, and sprouts in rows across the middle of the noodles. With your finger spread wasabi along the near edge of the nori. Carefully lift the edge of the mat closer to you and fold the nori over the filling, using a tucking and pulling motion so the sushi is firmly packed. Squeeze gently to make firmer. Unroll the mat and with a sharp, thin-bladed knife trim off either end. Slice the roll into 6 pieces. Repeat with the remaining nori and filling.

AHI AND JALAPEÑO MAKI

Yield: 18 pieces

3 sheets nori

1/2 cup (2 ounces) white Vinegar Rice
(page 28)

3 ounces (85 g) ahi or other tuna fillet,
cut in 1/2-inch (1.3-cm) strips

4-inch (10-cm) piece Japanese or
hothouse cucumber, peeled, halved,
seeded, and cut into 1/4 × 2-inch
(6 mm × 5-cm) strips

6 tablespoons (45 g) grated carrot

6 tablespoons (45 g) grated daikon

3 tablespoons thinly sliced scallion

1/2 jalapeño pepper, seeded and very
thinly sliced

1 1/2 teaspoons wasabi paste

To crisp the nori, toast sheets, shiny side down, over a flame or other direct heat. Place a sheet of nori on a bamboo sushi mat or cloth napkin, with the long side toward you. Divide all the remaining ingredients in three. Spread rice over the nori to within 1 inch (2.5 cm) of each long edge. Lay the ahi or tuna, cucumber, carrot, daikon, scallion, and jalapeño in rows across the middle of the rice. With your finger spread wasabi along the near edge of the nori. Carefully lift the edge of the mat closer to you and fold the nori over the filling, using a tucking and pulling motion so the sushi is firmly packed. Squeeze gently to make firmer. Unroll the mat and with a sharp, thin-bladed knife, trim off either end. Slice roll into six pieces. Repeat with the remaining nori and filling.

daikon

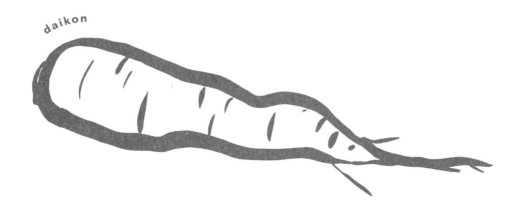

AHI, JÍCAMA, AND GINGER MAKI

Yield: 18 pieces

3 sheets nori
½ cup (2 ounces) brown Vinegar Rice
(page 28)
3 ounces (85 g) ahi or other tuna fillet,
cut in ½-inch (1.3-cm) strips
¼ ripe but firm avocado, thinly sliced
12 ¼ × 3-inch (6 mm × 7.5-cm) strips
jícama
9 snowpeas, blanched and split
lengthwise
3 teaspoons finely chopped gingerroot
1½ teaspoons wasabi paste

To crisp the nori, toast sheets, shiny side down, over a flame or other direct heat. Place a sheet of nori on a bamboo sushi mat or cloth napkin with the long side toward you. Divide all the remaining ingredients in three. Spread rice over the nori to within 1 inch (2.5 cm) of each long edge. Lay the ahi or tuna, avocado, jícama, snowpeas, and ginger in narrow rows across the middle of the rice. With your finger spread wasabi along the near edge of the nori. Carefully lift the edge of the mat closer to you and fold the nori over the filling, using a tucking and pulling motion so the sushi is firmly packed. Squeeze gently to make firmer. Unroll the mat and with a sharp, thin-bladed knife, trim off either end. Slice the roll into six pieces. Repeat with the remaining nori and filling.

ginger

SHRIMP AND AVOCADO MAKI

Yield: 18 pieces

3 sheets nori
½ cup (2 ounces) white Vinegar Rice
   (page 28)
6 cooked medium shrimp (prawns),
   peeled and split
¼ ripe but firm avocado, thinly sliced
12 basil leaves
3 tablespoons thinly sliced scallion
3 tablespoons chopped mint
1½ teaspoons wasabi paste

To crisp the nori, toast sheets, shiny side down, over a flame or other direct heat. Place a sheet of nori on a bamboo sushi mat or cloth napkin with the long side toward you. Divide all the remaining ingredients in three. Spread rice over the nori to within 1 inch (2.5 cm) of each long edge. Lay the shrimp, avocado, basil, scallion, and mint in narrow rows across the middle of the rice. With your finger spread wasabi along the near edge of the nori. Carefully lift the edge of the mat closer to you and fold the nori over the filling, using a tucking and pulling motion so the sushi is firmly packed. Squeeze gently to make firmer. Unroll the mat and with a sharp, thin-bladed knife, trim off either end. Slice the roll into six pieces. Repeat with the remaining nori and filling.

avocado

FRAGRANT ORANGE POT STICKERS

8 dried black mushrooms
1 bunch spinach (8 to 10 ounces/230 to
    280 g) or 4 ounces (115 g) frozen,
    washed and trimmed
4 tablespoons (60 ml) vegetable oil
2 teaspoons Asian sesame oil
3 cloves garlic, chopped
2-inch (5-cm) piece gingerroot, chopped
2 tablespoons chopped scallion
1 medium carrot, grated
8 ounces (230 g) firm tofu (soybean
    curd), rinsed and crumbled
Grated zest of 1/2 orange
2 tablespoons fresh orange juice
2 tablespoons soy sauce
2 tablespoons mirin
1 teaspoon salt
1 large egg white, beaten lightly
30 4-inch (10-cm) round wonton
    wrappers
Fragrant Orange Sauce (recipe follows)

To prevent these delectable Hong Kong–inspired dim sum from actually sticking, use a nonstick pan.

Yield: 30 dumplings

Soak the mushrooms in warm water 30 minutes. Drain and cut into 1/4-inch (6-mm) dice. Steam the spinach until just soft, about 15 seconds. Squeeze out as much liquid as possible and finely chop.

Heat 1 tablespoon of the vegetable oil and the sesame oil in a wok or medium sauté pan set over medium-high heat. Add the garlic, ginger, and scallion, and stir-fry 1 minute. Add the carrot and stir-fry 1 minute more, then fold in the tofu and cook 2 minutes. Stir in the spinach, mushrooms, orange zest, orange juice, soy sauce, mirin, and salt, and stir-fry 1 minute. Transfer to a bowl to cool. When cool, fold in the egg white.

Place 1 tablespoon of the filling in the center of each wonton wrapper. Moisten the edges with water and fold in half, pressing the edges to seal. Place the dumplings on a baking sheet lined with wax paper, cover with plastic wrap (cling film), and refrigerate 15 minutes.

Heat the remaining 3 tablespoons vegetable oil in a heavy sauté pan set over medium heat and cook the dumplings until they are dark brown on the bottom, about 6 minutes. Remove the dumplings and pour off the oil. Add the Fragrant Orange Sauce to the pan, return the dumplings, cover, and cook until the dumplings are translucent, about 2 minutes. Uncover and continue cooking until the sauce is reduced to a glaze, about 2 minutes. Serve the dumplings with the glaze spooned over them.

FRAGRANT ORANGE SAUCE

Yield: ¾ cup

½ cup (120 ml) chicken stock
2 tablespoons mirin
1 tablespoon oyster sauce
1 tablespoon finely chopped orange zest
1 tablespoon hoisin sauce
1 teaspoon Chinese chili sauce
1 teaspoon sugar

Put all the ingredients in a small bowl and whisk to combine.

orange

TROPICAL FRUIT–STUFFED VINE LEAVES

2 tablespoons vegetable oil

1 small onion, finely chopped

1 cup (140 g) rice

1 teaspoon salt

1 medium tomato, seeded and cut into
  small dice

¼ cup (60 g) small-dice fresh pineapple

1 banana, cut into small dice

1 cup (140 g) golden raisins (sultanas)

3 tablespoons finely chopped mint

2 tablespoons finely chopped sage

⅔ cup (85 g) roasted peanuts
  (groundnuts), coarsely chopped

1 teaspoon ground turmeric

1 teaspoon ground black pepper

28 vine leaves packed in brine, rinsed
  and dried

1 cup (250 ml) fruity white wine

1 cup (250 ml) vegetable stock

Juice of ½ lemon

3 tablespoons olive oil

Salt and ground black pepper

Lime wedges for garnish

These stuffed vine leaves take full advantage of the bounty and flavors of the tropics.

Yield: 24 pieces

Heat the oil in a medium, heavy saucepan set over medium-high heat and sauté the onion until soft, about 2 minutes. Stir in the rice and salt, and add water to cover.

Cover the pot and bring to a boil. Simmer until the water has been absorbed and the rice begins to soften.

Meanwhile, put the tomato, pineapple, banana, raisins, mint, sage, peanuts, turmeric, and pepper in a large bowl and mix well. When the rice is ready, add it to the fruit mixture and stir to combine.

Open a vine leaf on a flat surface, vein side up, and snip off the stem. Place about 2 tablespoons of the filling mixture in the center of the leaf and press it together with your hands. Fold the stem end up over the filling, fold in the sides, and roll the leaf into a small, tight parcel. Repeat with the remaining leaves. Place 3 or 4 flat vine leaves in the bottom of a medium pot and arrange the stuffed leaves in layers on top, packing them in tightly.

Combine the wine, stock, lemon juice, and olive oil, season with salt and pepper, and pour the mixture over the vine leaves. Place a plate on top of the stuffed leaves so they do not move during cooking. Simmer gently 45 minutes. Allow to cool, and serve garnished with lime wedges.

SCALLOPS IN LIME JUICE

1 cup (250 ml) freshly squeezed lime
    juice

½ cup (55 g) coarsely chopped Maui or
    Vidalia onion

3 teaspoons salt

2 pounds (900 g) sea scallops, cut into
    quarters

4 medium tomatoes, seeded and coarsely
    chopped

½ cup (55 g) thinly sliced scallion

2 tablespoons finely chopped cilantro
    (fresh coriander)

1 green bell pepper (capsicum), coarsely
    chopped

1 cup (250 ml) chilled coconut milk

This delicious island variation of seviche has a tropical flavor with the addition of coconut milk. I've used scallops here, but any firm-fleshed fish, such as ahi or swordfish, will work just as well.

Yield: 6 servings

In a deep, nonreactive bowl combine the lime juice, onion, and salt. Add the scallops and toss to coat. Cover tightly with plastic wrap (cling film) and refrigerate at least 3 hours, stirring occasionally. When they are ready, the scallops will be opaque and firm.

Just before serving, drain the scallops and toss with the tomatoes, scallion, cilantro, pepper, and coconut milk.

scallops

CHERRY TOMATOES FILLED WITH SALMON

24 large cherry tomatoes
3/4 cup (180 ml) fresh lime juice
1/2 cup (55 g) finely chopped scallion
1/4 teaspoon Tabasco (hot red sauce)
1 tablespoon salt
2 teaspoons ground black pepper
1 teaspoon sugar
1 1/2 pounds (675 g) salmon fillet, cut
  into 1/4-inch (6-mm) dice
2 medium tomatoes, peeled, seeded, and
  cut into 1/4-inch (6-mm) dice

This is a version of the popular local pupu lomi-lomi salmon. Lomi-lomi refers to the massagelike kneading method used when mixing the ingredients for this dish. Generally salted salmon is used, but many find the flavor too strong, so I've adjusted the traditional recipe by using fresh fish and tossing it gently in the marinade rather than kneading it.

Yield: 24 pieces

Cut off and discard the tops of the cherry tomatoes. Remove the pulp and discard. Place the tomatoes, cut side down, on a tray lined with paper towels (kitchen paper) and refrigerate until ready to use.

In a deep, nonreactive bowl combine the lime juice, scallion, Tabasco, salt, pepper, and sugar, and stir to mix. Add the salmon and turn gently to coat.

Cover the bowl with plastic wrap (cling film) and refrigerate about 5 hours, turning the fish occasionally. About 1 hour before serving, stir in the diced tomato. Just before serving, spoon the salmon mixture into the cherry tomatoes.

AHI SHOYU POKE

2 pounds (900 g) ahi cut into ¾-inch
   (2-cm) cubes
3 tablespoons grated gingerroot
¾ cup (85 g) finely chopped scallion
½ cup (120 ml) soy sauce
2 tablespoons toasted sesame seeds
1 head bok choy or romaine (cos)

No gathering in Hawaii would be complete without a few bowls of poke—raw fish cut into cubes and combined with different marinades. This is the most popular combination and is traditionally eaten with chopsticks. I like to serve the poke in palm-size leaves of bok choy or romaine.

Yield: 12 servings

Put the ahi, ginger, scallion, soy sauce, and sesame seeds in a bowl and stir well. To serve, tear leaves into comfortable holding sizes and spoon about 3 tablespoons of poke onto each piece.

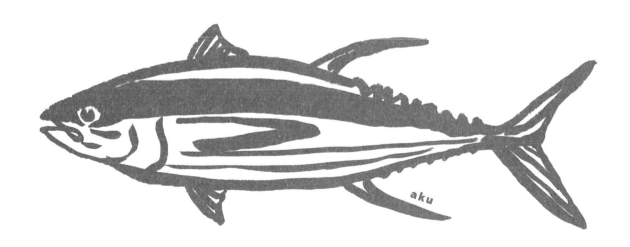

aku

CALAMARI RINGS

4 ounces (115 g) large spinach leaves,
    blanched
1/2 teaspoon wasabi paste
1 pound (450 g) medium-small squid,
    cleaned and tentacles removed and
    reserved
1 tablespoon lime juice
Salt
3 sheets nori
Lime wedges for garnish

Squid works wonderfully as a holder for interesting fillings. Serve these colorful appetizers with a squeeze of fresh lime juice.

Yield: about 20 rings

Spread the spinach leaves on paper towels (kitchen paper) and pat dry. Place 2 or 3 leaves together to match the length of the squid body. Spread a small amount of wasabi down the center of the leaves. Lay the squid tentacles down the center of the leaves, squeeze lime juice over them, and sprinkle with salt. Roll up into a tight tube. To crisp the nori, toast sheets, shiny side down, over a flame or other direct heat. Cut it to match the length of the tube, then tightly roll up the tube in the nori.

Stuff the tube into the cavity of the squid and fasten with a toothpick. Repeat with the remaining ingredients. Arrange the stuffed squid in one layer in a steamer, cover, and cook about 6 minutes until opaque. Allow to cool, then refrigerate until cold. Cut into 3/4-inch (2-cm) slices and serve garnished with lime wedges.

squid

TOMATOES STUFFED WITH GOAT CHEESE

Yield: 12 pieces

12 small tomatoes
2 cloves garlic, peeled
12 ounces (340 g) crumbly goat cheese
   (chèvre)
1/2 cup (20 g) loosely packed basil
1/3 cup (80 ml) olive oil
1 tablespoon freshly squeezed lime juice
1/3 cup (40 g) pine nuts (pine kernels)
Vegetable oil for greasing pan

Preheat the oven to 350°F (175°C). Cut the tops off the tomatoes and reserve. Scoop out and discard the pulp. Chop the garlic fine in a food processor by dropping the cloves into the bowl with the motor running. Add the goat cheese, basil, olive oil, and lime juice, and process until blended. Lightly toast the pine nuts in a small, heavy pan. Fill the tomatoes with the goat-cheese mixture and top with pine nuts. Place the tops on the tomatoes, arrange them on a lightly greased baking sheet, and cook 15 to 18 minutes, or until the tomatoes are soft. Let cool slightly before serving.

COCONUT MEATBALLS

Yield: about 20 meatballs

1 pound (450 g) lean ground (minced)
   beef
4 cups (360 g) grated coconut
1 egg
2 tablespoons finely chopped cilantro
   (fresh coriander)
2 cloves garlic, finely chopped
3 teaspoons ground coriander
1 teaspoon ground cumin
2 teaspoons salt
1 teaspoon ground black pepper
Vegetable oil for deep-frying
Fresh pineapple chunks for garnish

Put the beef, coconut, egg, cilantro, garlic, coriander, cumin, salt, and pepper in a deep bowl, and knead until well combined. Form meatballs of about 1/4 cup (4 tablespoons) each. Heat oil in a large, heavy pan set over medium heat until it is very hot but not smoking. Deep-fry the meatballs, 5 or 6 at a time, until they are crisp and nicely browned. Drain on paper towels (kitchen paper) and keep warm until ready to serve. To serve, put each meatball on a small bamboo skewer with a piece of pineapple.

VINE LEAVES STUFFED WITH SQUASH, HUMMUS, AND TABBOULEH

12 brine-packed vine leaves
1 cup (460 g) Hummus (page 198)
1 cup (280 g) Tabbouleh (recipe follows)
1 cup (280 g) mashed cooked acorn
   squash or pumpkin purée

Squash is eaten widely throughout the tropics. Here, combined with the traditional Middle Eastern dishes hummus and tabbouleh, it becomes a very exotic "East meets East" pupu.

Yield: 12 pieces

Open a vine leaf on a flat surface, vein side up, and snip off the stems. Place 2 heaping teaspoons of hummus in the center of the leaf. Place 2 heaping teaspoons of tabbouleh on the hummus, pressing down so the grains stick to the paste. Top with 2 teaspoons of squash. Fold the stem end up over the filling, fold in the sides, and roll up. Repeat with the remaining leaves. Serve chilled.

TABBOULEH

½ cup (200 g) bulgur
⅓ cup (40 g) finely chopped scallion
⅓ cup (15 g) finely chopped parsley
3 tablespoons finely chopped mint
2 tablespoons olive oil
2 tablespoons freshly squeezed
   lemon juice
Salt and ground black pepper

Yield: 2 cups

Soak the bulgur in 1 cup (250 ml) cold water about 30 minutes, or until soft. Drain and squeeze out as much water as possible. Refrigerate at least 30 minutes before using. Add the scallion, parsley, mint, oil, and lemon juice, season with salt and pepper, and mix to combine.

BLACK BEAN AND FETA QUESADILLA

Yield: 4 quesadillas

15-ounce (525-g) can black beans, drained
1 medium onion, finely chopped
12 kalamata olives, pitted and chopped
½ cup (20 g) chopped parsley
1 jalapeño pepper, seeded and finely chopped
½ teaspoon cayenne
½ teaspoon paprika
2 teaspoons ground cumin
½ cup (55 g) pine nuts (pine kernels)
8 whole-wheat tortillas
4 ounces (115 g) feta cheese, crumbled
¼ cup (55 g) capers
Shredded lettuce and mustard, clover, or radish sprouts for garnish

Put the beans, onion, olives, parsley, jalapeño, cayenne, paprika, and cumin in a food processor, pulse, then process until combined but still chunky. Heat a small, heavy pan over medium-high heat. Lightly toast the pine nuts and set aside.

Place a tortilla on a flat surface. Spread with a quarter of the bean mixture and top with 1 ounce of the feta, 1 tablespoon of the capers, and 2 tablespoons of the pine nuts. Place a tortilla on top and press down gently.

Carefully lift the quesadilla and place it in the preheated pan. Cook until the beans are heated through and the tortilla is browned, about 3 minutes. Turn and brown the other side. Repeat with the remaining ingredients.

Cut each quesadilla into 6 wedges and top with shredded lettuce and sprouts.

PACIFIC CHICKEN SALAD TARTLETS

Yield: 30 tartlets

2 tablespoons soy sauce

2 tablespoons mirin

$^1/_4$ cup (60 ml) macadamia nut or
   peanut oil

$^1/_4$ cup (60 ml) vegetable oil

2 tablespoons Asian sesame oil

$^1/_4$ cup (4 tablespoons) finely chopped
   cilantro (fresh coriander)

3 scallions, finely chopped

$1^1/_2$ pounds (675 g) cooked skinless,
   boneless chicken breast, chilled and
   cut into $^1/_4$-inch (6-mm) dice

1 medium ripe but firm papaya
   (pawpaw), cut into $^1/_4$-inch (6-mm)
   dice

Tartlet Shells (recipe follows)

Combine the soy sauce, mirin, nut oil, vegetable oil, sesame oil, cilantro, and scallion in a large bowl. Add the chicken and papaya, and stir to coat. Spoon the mixture into the Tartlet Shells and serve immediately.

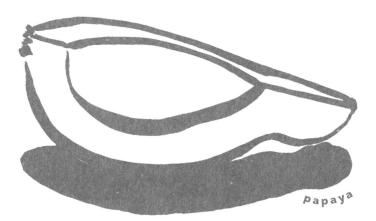

papaya

TARTLET SHELLS

2 cups (280 g) all-purpose (plain) flour
1/4 teaspoon salt
8 tablespoons (1 stick) (115 g) cold
    unsalted butter, cut into 8 pieces
2 eggs, lightly beaten
Vegetable oil for greasing pans

These thin pastry shells are ideal for cocktail parties and work well with a variety of fillings.

Pulse the flour and salt in a food processor a few times to combine. Add the butter, pulse a few times, then process until the mixture resembles bread crumbs. With the machine running, add the eggs and process until the dough just begins to pull away from the sides of the bowl. Transfer the dough to a lightly floured surface, form it into a disc, wrap it in plastic wrap (cling film), and refrigerate about 30 minutes.

Preheat the oven to 400°F (200°C). Lightly grease 30 3-inch (7.5-cm) tart pans. (If you have fewer tart pans, repeat rolling and cooking process as many times as necessary.)

Roll the dough out 1/8-inch (3-mm) thick on a lightly floured surface and cut into 30 circles with a 4-inch (10-cm) round pastry cutter. Press it into the pans and trim off any excess. Put the pans on a baking sheet and prick the dough all over with a fork.

Bake 10 to 15 minutes, or until golden. Cool on racks, then remove from pans.

BRUNCH

BRUNCH

is a popular island
tradition. Hotel guests and
locals alike can be found min-
gling around buffet tables and
lining up at omelette bars at the
many lavish oceanfront resorts. Festive occasions such as weddings and
birthdays are often celebrated with a
brunch. The most Hawaiian of these
occasions is the Baby Luau, a huge
celebration honoring a child's
first birthday. All the aunties,
uncles, cousins, grand-
parents, friends, and
neighbors

are invited, and the occasion is treated with much the same reverence as a wedding.

Egg dishes are a must at brunch. Included here are a selection of both new recipes and old-fashioned recipes modernized with the addition of exotic fresh herbs. With fish and poultry often replacing red meat today, we offer Pacific Eggs Benedict (page 53), a pan-Pacific version of eggs Benedict, with smoked fish instead of the traditional ham and topped with an easy-to-make Cilantro-Lime Hollandaise (page 199).

The Brunch Torte (page 54) brings together a spectacular assemblage of breakfast foods and has the added advantage of being able to be made up to a day in advance. This truly exceptional dish combines various contrasting layers of color and texture with unique and delicious tastes. It is a perfect dish for a buffet, as it can be warmed just before serving, removed from the pan, and sliced, keeping the shape intact to show off the layers of contrasting bright colors.

For serving large groups of people, Baked Eggs with Spinach in Crumb Crust (page 56), a variation of eggs Florentine, works particularly well. The crust and spinach mixture can be prepared up to 2 days in advance, and large trays of eggs can be baked at the same time just before serving.

Brunch would not be complete without muffins. I like to serve small muffins in different flavors for variety, mixing plain muffins, such as corn, whole grain, or bran, with spicy muffins, such as ginger and cinnamon, or fruity muffins, such as papaya-banana.

Many popular brunch items can be made in advance, which is a big advantage, as brunch starts early in the day. The more you can do in advance, the less you need to rush around frantically just before the party, and the more time you will have to relax and enjoy your guests and your food.

Have all your serving platters ready the day before, and, if you can, set your table the night before. You may also want to set up the bar a day in advance, so all you'll need to do is add ice.

CITRUS MUFFINS WITH SMOKED TURKEY AND GUAVA JELLY

Butter for greasing pans
2 cups (280 g) all-purpose (plain) flour
1 teaspoon baking soda (bicarbonate
*   of soda)*
1 teaspoon salt
1 cup Demerara or turbinado sugar or
*   light brown sugar*
8 tablespoons (1 stick) (115 g) cold
*   unsalted butter, cut into 8 pieces*
2 large eggs
1 cup (250 ml) buttermilk
Zest of ¹/₂ orange
Zest of ¹/₂ lime
¹/₄ cup (60 ml) freshly squeezed
*   orange juice*
1 cup (140 g) golden raisins (sultanas)
1 tablespoon freshly squeezed lemon juice
1 tablespoon freshly squeezed lime juice
¹/₂ cup (115 g) guava or other tropical
*   fruit jelly*
¹/₂ pound (230 g) thinly sliced smoked
*   turkey*

Smoked turkey, called kalua turkey, is very popular in the islands, where whole turkeys are salted, wrapped in ti leaves or banana leaves, and placed in the imu (roasting pit) alongside the pig, fish, ulu (breadfruit), taro, and sweet potatoes. Smoked chicken or duck work equally well with these muffins, as does any tropical fruit jelly.

Yield: 24 mini-muffins

Preheat the oven to 400°F (200°C) and lightly butter pans for 24 mini-muffins.

Combine the flour, baking soda, and salt in a large mixing bowl and set aside. Put the sugar and cold butter in a food processor, pulse, then process until smooth. With the motor running, add the eggs one at a time. Add the buttermilk and pulse to combine, stopping to scrape down the sides of the bowl as necessary. Add the orange and lime zests and the orange juice, and pulse to combine. Add the flour mixture and pulse until just moistened. Stir in the raisins.

Pour the batter into the muffin pans, filling them to the top. Bake until the muffins are golden brown, about 15 minutes.

Combine the lemon and lime juice and brush the mixture over the top of the warm muffins. Let sit 5 minutes, then remove the muffins from the pan and allow to cool completely.

Cut each muffin in half, spread the bottom half with a thin layer of jelly, top with a piece of smoked turkey, and replace the muffin top.

PACIFIC EGGS BENEDICT

4 English muffins or crumpets, split
8 ounces (230 g) smoked salmon or
    smoked ahi (tuna)
8 eggs
Cilantro-Lime Hollandaise (page 199)
4 thin lime slices for garnish
4 cilantro sprigs for garnish

You could use any smoked fish for this Pacific island version of the popular brunch standard, but I've found that it is a big hit when made with either ahi or salmon. The hollandaise and poached eggs can be made up to an hour ahead and kept warm in a pan of hot water in a 250°F (120°C) oven. Garnish with cilantro sprigs, so your guests can recognize the unexpected flavor in the sauce.

Yield: 4 servings

Toast the muffins. Place some smoked fish on each muffin half.

To poach the eggs, butter the bottom of a 6- to 8-inch (15- to 20-cm) saucepan. Fill the pan with about 1 inch (2.5 cm) of water, add a little salt, and bring to a boil. While the water comes to a boil, crack open an egg in the pan and slide the egg into the center of the well formed by the swirling water. Reduce the heat to low and simmer the egg for about 4 minutes, or until the white is firm and the yolk is still soft. Remove with a slotted spoon and drain on paper towels (kitchen paper). Repeat for the remaining eggs. If not serving immediately, plunge the egg into ice water. To reheat, bring a pot of water to a boil, remove from heat, and place the cooked egg into hot water for about 2 minutes before serving. Drain well

Place a poached egg on top of each fish-topped muffin half. Pour hollandaise over the center of the eggs, garnish each serving with a cilantro sprig and a slice of lime, and serve immediately.

BRUNCH TORTE

THE EGG-AND-CHEESE LAYER

12 eggs
1/2 cup (120 ml) milk
1 teaspoon salt
1/2 teaspoon ground black pepper
1/2 cup (20 g) parsley leaves
4 tablespoons (1/2 stick) (55 g) unsalted
    butter
4 ounces (115 g) Swiss cheese, grated
4 ounces (115 g) Parmesan cheese, grated

THE PEPPER LAYER

3 red bell peppers (capsicums)

THE TURKEY LAYER

1 pound (450 g) smoked turkey breast,
    cut into 1-inch (2.5-cm) cubes
2 tablespoons Dijon mustard
2 large egg whites

THE SPINACH LAYER

2 pounds (900 g) chopped spinach or
    2 10-ounce bags (280 g each) frozen
1/2 medium onion, peeled and quartered
3 cloves garlic, peeled
2 tablespoons unsalted butter
2 large egg whites
1/2 teaspoon cayenne
1 teaspoon salt
1/2 teaspoon ground black pepper

THE ASSEMBLY

Butter for greasing pan

The contrasting layers of colors and textures in this dish make it a perfect brunch item, even if the ingredients are not particularly Pacific Rim (except for the spinach, which is eaten throughout the area). Simpler to prepare than it looks, this torte can be assembled a day in advance and baked just before serving. In fact, preparing it in advance gives the layers a chance to settle and hold their shape.

Yield: 8 to 10 servings

Put the eggs, milk, salt, pepper, and parsley in a bowl and whisk to blend. Heat the butter in a large, heavy pan set over medium-low heat and add the egg mixture. When almost cooked through but still runny, remove from the heat and stir in three-quarters of the Swiss cheese and three-quarters of the Parmesan cheese. Refrigerate the eggs until needed.

Char the peppers over a gas flame or under a broiler until blackened all over. Put them in a sealed paper bag. When they are cool, peel, seed, and quarter them.

Put the turkey cubes in a food processor and pulse to coarsely chop. (You may have to do this in batches; check the instructions of your food processor.) Add the mustard and egg whites, and process briefly to mix. Transfer the mixture to a bowl and refrigerate until ready to use.

Blanche the spinach and refresh under cold water. Squeeze to remove as much liquid as possible, and set aside. With the motor running, drop the onion and garlic into a food processor and process until finely chopped. (Do not wash the processor bowl between steps.) Heat the butter in a small sauté pan set over medium heat and cook the garlic and onion until they are soft but not browned. Transfer to the food processor and add the spinach, egg whites, cayenne, salt, and pepper. Pulse a few times, then process to purée, stopping to scrape down the sides of the bowl as necessary. Cover and refrigerate until ready to use.

To assemble the torte, preheat the oven to 400°F (200°C). Butter an 8-inch (20-cm) springform pan. Put half the egg mixture in the pan and spread it evenly with a spatula. Cover with half the spinach mixture, smoothing and packing it down with the spatula. Next add all the turkey mixture. Arrange the red peppers evenly over the turkey, making sure they reach the edges of the pan. Top the pepper layer with the remaining spinach, then the remaining egg mixture, pressing down firmly between each layer. Sprinkle the top with the rest of the cheeses. (If preparing a day in advance, cover tightly with plastic wrap and refrigerate. Remove ½ hour before baking.)

Bake 30 minutes. Remove from oven and let rest 30 minutes. Carefully run a thin knife blade around the sides of the pan, remove the springform, and transfer the torte on its pan bottom to a serving platter. To serve, cut in wedges.

bell pepper

BAKED EGGS WITH SPINACH IN CRUMB CRUST

THE CRUST

8 tablespoons (1 stick) (115 g) unsalted
   butter plus more for greasing pan
12 slices white bread
1/2 teaspoon salt
1/4 teaspoon ground black pepper
2 large egg whites

THE SPINACH MIXTURE

8 ounces (230 g) chopped spinach or
   1/2 10-ounce bag frozen, thawed
1 medium onion, finely chopped
Salt and ground black pepper
2 ounces (55 g) cream cheese, at room
   temperature

12 large eggs

This eye-catching dish is especially good for large gatherings, as most of the preparation can be done up to two days in advance. For a sit-down brunch, figure 2 eggs per person and serve with a spicy chicken herb or turkey sausage. For a buffet, allow 1 egg per person and arrange them on a bed of fresh herbs on large platters surrounded with sliced sausage.

Yield: 12 baked eggs

Preheat the oven to 400°F (200°C) and butter pans for 12 large (3 1/2 × 2-inch [8.9 × 5-cm]) muffins.

Cut the bread in quarters and coarsely chop it in a food processor. (Do not wash out the bowl.) Spread the crumbs out on a baking sheet and bake 10 minutes. Remove from the oven and let cool. (Do not turn off the oven.)

Return the bread crumbs to the processor bowl, add 6 tablespoons of the butter, the salt, and the pepper and pulse several times to combine. Beat the 2 egg whites until stiff and fold into the crumb mixture.

Divide the mixture among the prepared muffin cups and press it against the bottom and sides to form an even crust. (The crusts can be prepared up to 2 days ahead and refrigerated, covered with plastic wrap [cling film].)

If using frozen spinach, squeeze to remove as much liquid as possible. Heat the remaining 2 tablespoons butter in a medium sauté pan set over medium-high heat and cook the onion until it is soft but not browned. Add the spinach, season with salt and pepper, stir, and cook until heated through, about 6 minutes. Transfer the mixture to a food processor and pulse several times to mix. Add the cream cheese and process until smooth. (The spinach mixture can be prepared up to 2 days ahead and refrigerated in a covered container.)

Place the eggs in very hot, but not boiling, water, cover, and let stand 10 minutes.

Meanwhile, bake the crusts 6 minutes. Remove from the oven (do not turn off the oven), divide the spinach mixture evenly among the crusts, and press it around the sides with the back of a spoon to form a cup. Crack an egg into each spinach-filled crust. Return the pan to the oven and bake 5 minutes, or until the whites are set and the yolks still runny. Run a thin knife blade around each crust, lift gently, and transfer to a platter. Serve immediately.

SPICED PUMPKIN FRITTERS

1/2 cup (100 g) plus 1 tablespoon sugar
1 tablespoon ground cinnamon
2/3 cup (160 ml) milk
2 large eggs
1 tablespoon vegetable oil
1/2 teaspoon vanilla extract
2/3 cup (95 g) all-purpose (plain) flour
1/2 teaspoon salt
1 teaspoon baking powder
1 cup (460 g) cooked pumpkin purée
Vegetable oil for frying

Many types of squash and gourds are grown for both food and decoration throughout the Pacific. This recipe can be made with pumpkin or butternut, Hubbard, or acorn squash. These sweet fritters can be served as a breakfast treat with coffee and fruit or for dessert.

Yield: about 20 3-inch (7.5-cm) fritters

Combine the 1/2 cup (100 g) sugar and the cinnamon, and set aside.

Put the milk, eggs, oil, and vanilla in a food processor and process just to combine. Add the flour, salt, the 1 tablespoon sugar, and the baking powder, and process 10 seconds more. Add the pumpkin purée and process about 15 seconds, stopping to scrape down the sides of the bowl as necessary. Cover and refrigerate at least 30 minutes.

Put enough oil in a large, heavy sauté pan to cover the bottom, and heat the oil over medium heat. Stir the batter and drop it by heaping tablespoons into the pan, without crowding. Cook each side until browned, about 2 minutes. Remove the fritters with a slotted spatula as they are done and place on paper towels (kitchen paper). Keep warm in a low oven. Just before serving, sprinkle on both sides with the cinnamon-sugar mixture.

COCONUT-CORN FRITTERS

1/4 cup (60 ml) coconut milk
1 cinnamon stick
2 tablespoons unsalted butter
2 tablespoons sugar
2 cups (230 g) corn (maize) kernels
1/4 cup (35 g) corn (maize) flour
1 large egg
Vegetable oil for frying
Warm honey or cream cheese

Some of the sweetest corn is grown on the lush tropical mountain slopes on the windward side of the island, with its sun-filled days and tropical rain-drenched nights. Corn was incorporated into the foods of the islands when the paniolos, or cowboys, immigrated from Mexico to work on the upcountry cattle ranches.

Yield: about 16 3-inch (7.5-cm) fritters

Put the coconut milk and cinnamon in a saucepan set over medium heat and bring to a boil. Reduce the heat and simmer 5 minutes. Add the butter and sugar, and stir until the butter has melted. Remove from the heat, let sit 10 minutes, then remove and discard the cinnamon stick.

Put 1 cup (115 g) of the corn kernels in a food processor and process to purée. Add the flour, egg, and coconut milk, and process 10 seconds. Transfer the mixture to a bowl and stir in the remaining 1 cup (115 g) corn kernels. Cover and refrigerate at least 30 minutes.

Coat the bottom of a large, heavy sauté pan with oil and heat over medium heat. Stir the batter and drop it by heaping tablespoonfuls into the pan, without crowding. Cook until golden brown on both sides, about 2 minutes per side. Keep warm in a low oven. Serve with warmed honey or cream cheese.

ZUCCHINI FRITTERS

1 pound (450 g) zucchini (courgettes),
  grated
2 cups (230 g) sliced scallion
1/2 cup (20 g) mint
1/2 cup (20 g) cilantro (fresh coriander)
1/2 teaspoon salt
1/4 teaspoon ground black pepper
3 large eggs, beaten
4 ounces (115 g) raw cashews, ground
4 ounces (115 g) soft goat cheese
  (chèvre)
Olive oil for frying
Yogurt-Cucumber Sauce (page 199)

These fluffy fritters owe their refreshing flavor to the combination of mint and cilantro.

Yield: about 24 3-inch (7.5-cm) fritters

Put the grated zucchini in paper towels (kitchen paper) and wring to remove as much liquid as possible. Repeat with another towel if necessary.

Transfer to a large bowl, add the scallion, mint, cilantro, salt, and pepper, and stir to combine. Stir in the eggs and then the ground cashews. Add the goat cheese and stir again. Cover and refrigerate at least 30 minutes.

Coat the bottom of a large, heavy sauté pan with oil and heat over medium-high heat. Drop the zucchini mixture into the pan by heaping tablespoons and cook until golden brown on both sides, about 3 minutes per side. Keep warm in a low oven. Serve with Yogurt-Cucumber Sauce.

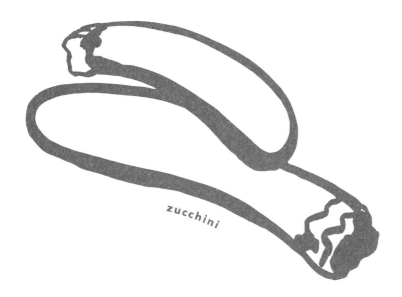

zucchini

SWEET POTATO FRITTERS WITH GOAT CHEESE

FRITTERS

1 pound (450 g) sweet potatoes, peeled and grated

¹/₂ cup (55 g) thinly sliced scallion

¹/₂ teaspoon salt

¹/₄ teaspoon ground black pepper

4 tablespoons (60 ml) olive oil

4 ounces (115 g) crumbly goat cheese (chèvre)

SALAD

1¹/₂ tablespoons freshly squeezed lime juice

3 tablespoons macadamia nut or walnut oil

¹/₂ teaspoon salt

¹/₄ teaspoon ground black pepper

12 ounces (345 g) mesclun

Delicious and simple to prepare, these crisp, bright-orange-and-green fritters with their creamy white filling look festive presented on a plate of baby mesclun greens.

Yield: 8 fritters

Combine the sweet potato, scallion, salt, and pepper in a bowl. Heat 1 tablespoon of the olive oil in a large, heavy pan set over medium heat. Mound ¹/₄ cup (4 tablespoons) of the sweet potato mixture in the pan and flatten it with a spatula to form a 3-inch (7.5-cm) round. Repeat to make 3 more patties. Cook 3 minutes, then turn. Top each of 2 patties with one-eighth of the goat cheese, cover with the remaining 2 patties, and press to seal. Cook until the bottom is crisp and browned, about 3 minutes, then turn to brown other side. Repeat the process with the remaining olive oil and sweet potato mixture to make a total of 8 fritters.

Whisk together the lime juice, nut oil, salt, and pepper. Toss the mesclun greens in the dressing, divide the salad among 4 plates, and top each with 2 fritters.

SHRIMP FRITTERS

½ cup (120 ml) water
1 teaspoon paprika
1 teaspoon salt
12 large shrimp (prawns), peeled and
    deveined
1 cup (140 g) all-purpose (plain) flour
1 cup (140 g) cornstarch (cornflour)
1 large sweet potato (about ½ pound/
    230 g), coarsely grated
1 medium acorn (winter) squash,
    coarsely grated
Vegetable oil for deep-frying
½ cup (55 g) finely chopped scallion
Garlic Sauce (recipe follows)

Put the water, paprika, and salt in a medium saucepan and bring to a boil. Add the shrimp and turn off the heat. Cover and let sit 2 minutes, or until the shrimp are firm and pink; do not overcook. Remove the shrimp with a slotted spoon, reserving the cooking liquid, and drain on paper towels (kitchen paper).

Pour the liquid into a 2-cup (500-ml) glass measure and add enough water to make 1¼ cups (310 ml).

Sift the flour and cornstarch into a large bowl, add the 1¼ cups (310 ml) shrimp liquid, and stir until the liquid has been absorbed. Add the sweet potato and squash, and stir to combine.

Pour oil to a depth of ½ inch (1.3 cm) into a heavy, 10-inch (25-cm) sauté pan set over medium heat and heat until the oil is very hot but not smoking. Pour ⅓ cup (80 ml) of the vegetable batter onto a saucer to make a 2½-inch (6.4-cm) fritter, sprinkle with 2 teaspoons scallion, and lightly press a shrimp into the center. Holding the saucer close to the surface of the hot oil, slide the fritter into the oil with the aid of a spatula. Repeat with remaining batter, scallion, and shrimp.

Cook (in batches, if necessary) until richly browned on both sides, about 3 minutes per side, turning them carefully. Drain on paper towels (kitchen paper) and keep warm in a low oven. Just before serving, brush with a little Garlic Sauce.

GARLIC SAUCE

6 cloves garlic, finely chopped
1 teaspoon salt
1 cup (250 ml) Japanese rice-wine
    vinegar

Yield: 1 cup (250 ml)

Using the back of a spoon or a mortar and pestle, crush the garlic with the salt to form a smooth paste. Stir in the vinegar. Refrigerate, tightly covered, until ready to use.

garlic

SOUPS

OUR tour of the Pacific offers many delicious soups—from cool, spicy gazpacho to earthy, rich wild-mushroom broth; from aromatic and exotic coconut and lemongrass flavors and hot-and-sour, peppery, and vinegary soups to soulful seafood chowders and bouillabaisse teeming with ocean treasures of scallops, lobster, mussels, and shrimp floating in a sea of fragrant, herb-scented liquid. Every country or region boasts its specialties, from potent potages served up at street-market stalls in Southeast Asia, with brisk flavors that jump out of the bowl, to thin liquids filled with colorful julienne vegetables swimming around translucent noodles in Japan. This selection of soups not only takes us through the Pacific, stopping at exotic ports of call, but also explores familiar favorites modernized with unexpected twists.

A stop in Mexico inspires Pacific Black Bean Soup (page 68), with its orange and coriander flavors. From Thailand comes the subtly fragrant Opal-Basil Coconut Soup (page 69), scented with lemon grass and ginger. Usually associated with Italian food, basil is actually native to Southeast Asia. The Thais use a number of different basils with distinct flavors as diverse as cinnamon, lemon, and licorice. A pan-Pacific version of a French classic, Vegetable Soup with Cilantro Pesto (page 70), highlights another herb popular throughout the Pacific.

For lovers of cold soup, and especially vichyssoise, there is the silky-smooth Ulussoise (page 72), made with breadfruit, or ulu, a staple throughout the Pacific.

Another soup equally delicious served hot or chilled is Sweet Potato and Pear Bisque (page 73). The delectable Seafood Soup with coconut, macadamia nuts, and gingerroot (page 74), brimming with seafood and fresh fish, is based on the Brazilian specialty vatapá. From Hong Kong comes the popular Hot-and-Sour Shrimp Soup (page 75), here elevated above the ordinary with the addition of lemon grass and rice wine.

For a light and especially tasty spin on onion soup, try Maui Onion Soup with Goat Cheese Toasts (page 76). Goat cheese, with its subtle hint of fresh grass and lemony overtones, has been embraced by the island population in the past few years, and we rarely see a menu that doesn't feature at least one dish made with it.

Allow these recipes to introduce you to new foods and flavors. Adjust seasonings and spices to your taste, and then share your savory soups with friends.

TROPICAL GAZPACHO

3 English (hothouse) cucumbers, peeled and cut into ¼-inch (6-mm) dice

6 medium tomatoes, peeled, seeded, and cut into ¼-inch (6-mm) dice

1 green bell pepper (capsicum), cut into ¼-inch (6-mm) dice

1 red bell pepper (capsicum), cut into ¼-inch (6-mm) dice

1 large Maui or Vidalia (sweet) onion, cut into ¼-inch (6-mm) dice

5 cloves garlic, finely chopped

4 cups (230 g) coarsely torn crustless French bread

1½-inch (4-cm) piece gingerroot, grated

4 cups (1 l) very cold water

¼ cup (60 ml) mirin

¼ cup (60 ml) white-wine vinegar

1 tablespoon freshly squeezed lime juice

1 tablespoon salt

½ cup (120 ml) extra-virgin olive oil

½ cup (20 g) coarsely chopped cilantro (fresh coriander)

½ cup (55 g) thinly sliced scallion

½ cup (55 g) grated jícama

2 ounces (55 g) enoki mushrooms

Cold soups are ideally suited to the tropics, and gazpacho is one of the all-time favorites. With its hints of cilantro, lime, and ginger, this version is representative of the Pacific. Guests can choose from an array of garnishes to suit their tastes. Serve with a crisp white wine.

Yield: 6 servings

Reserve ½ cup each of the cucumber, tomato, and green and red bell peppers combined, and set aside for garnish. Put the remaining cucumber, tomato, green pepper, red pepper, onion, garlic, and bread in a food processor. Pulse a few times, then process to purée.

Squeeze the grated ginger in a fine-mesh sieve to extract the juice, discarding the pulp. Add the ginger juice, water, mirin, white-wine vinegar, lime juice, and salt to the vegetable purée, and process a few seconds to blend. With the motor running, add the oil in a steady stream. Transfer the soup to a large bowl, cover tightly with plastic wrap (cling film), and refrigerate at least 2 hours.

Adjust the seasoning with vinegar and salt, and sprinkle with the cilantro. Serve surrounded by small bowls of the diced cucumber, tomato, and peppers, and the jícama and enoki mushrooms.

enoki mushrooms

PACIFIC BLACK BEAN SOUP

2 15-ounce (525-g) cans black beans
3 cups (750 ml) chicken stock
1 teaspoon ground Szechwan pepper
1 tablespoon Asian sesame oil
4 cloves garlic, chopped
2 cups (230 g) coarsely chopped onion
2 cups (230 g) coarsely chopped carrot
1/2 cup (55 g) coarsely chopped celery
3 jalapeño peppers, seeded and chopped
2 tablespoons ground cumin
1 tablespoon ground coriander
2 teaspoons salt
1/4 cup (60 ml) freshly squeezed
  orange juice
1 1/2 tablespoons grated orange zest
4 to 6 ounces (115 to 170 g) Monterey
  Jack cheese, grated
1 avocado, thinly sliced
Cilantro (fresh coriander) for garnish

Inspired by Mexican dishes combining beans, cheese, and avocado, this beautifully presented variation of black bean soup is given a tropical note with the addition of orange and coriander.

Yield: 4 to 6 servings

Put the beans and their liquid in a large saucepan set over medium heat. Add 2 cups (500 ml) of the chicken stock and the pepper, and bring to a boil. Reduce the heat and simmer while you prepare the vegetables.

In a large, heavy sauté pan set over medium-high heat, heat the oil and sauté the garlic and onion until soft but not browned, about 5 minutes. Add the carrots, celery, jalapeño, cumin, coriander, and salt. Stir in the remaining 1 cup (250 ml) stock, lower the heat, cover, and simmer until the vegetables are soft, about 10 minutes. Purée the vegetable mixture in a food processor or blender.

Add the orange juice and zest, and process to combine. Add 2 cups (500 ml) of the bean-and-stock mixture and process until smooth. Stir the purée into the remaining beans and stock and reheat. Ladle the soup into bowls, top each with 1 ounce grated cheese and avocado slices, and garnish with cilantro leaves.

OPAL-BASIL COCONUT SOUP

4 cups (1 l) coconut milk

1 cup (250 ml) water

4-ounce (115-g) can sliced water
   chestnuts, drained, liquid reserved

1/4 cup (55 g) white miso paste

9-inch (23-cm) stalk lemon grass cut into
   3 pieces or zest of 1/2 lemon in strips

4 kaffir lime leaves or zest of 1/2 lime
   in strips

2-inch (5-cm) piece gingerroot, thinly
   sliced

8-ounce (230 g) can straw mushrooms,
   drained

8-ounce (230-g) can miniature corn,
   drained and split

1 pound (450 g) medium silken tofu
   (soybean curd), cut into 1/2-inch
   (1.3-cm) cubes

1 cup (40 g) tightly packed basil,
   shredded

Salt

1/2 cup (120 ml) freshly squeezed
   lime juice

With the addition of tofu, this fragrant soup is richer in protein and iron than red meat and very high in calcium and vitamin C.

Yield: 4 to 6 servings

Put the coconut milk, water, and reserved liquid from the water chestnuts in a large saucepan set over medium heat. When heated through, stir in the miso paste. Add the lemon grass, lime leaves, and ginger, and bring to a boil. Add the water chestnuts, mushrooms, and corn. Reduce the heat, add the tofu and basil, season with salt, and simmer 10 minutes. Just before serving, remove the lemon grass and lime leaves (or zests) and stir in the lime juice.

straw mushrooms

VEGETABLE SOUP WITH CILANTRO PESTO

THE PESTO

¼ cup (50 g) raw cashew nuts
¼ cup (50 g) roasted cashew nuts
4 cloves garlic, peeled
1 cup (40 g) cilantro (fresh coriander)
½ cup (120 ml) olive oil
½ cup (55 g) grated Parmesan cheese

THE STOCK

4 cloves garlic
1 tablespoon coarsely chopped gingerroot
4 sprigs thyme
1 teaspoon cumin seeds
1 teaspoon fennel seeds
4 cups (1 l) cold water
2 3-inch (7.5-cm) pieces celery
(continued on next page)

Made with an assortment of fresh vegetables that follow a loose formula of one green vegetable, one type of fresh bean, one type of dry bean, potatoes, and tomatoes, this is a hearty variation of the lovely French soup. Served as a main course with a simple salad and crusty slices of warm bread, this unusual soup will have your guests holding their bowls out for more. Similar to Italian pesto, this has a Pacific Asian twist—cashews have been substituted for the pine nuts and coriander for basil. Just before serving, the creamy green pesto is placed in the bottom of the soup tureen and stirred into the hot soup to release its rich aroma.

Yield: 4 to 6 servings

To make the pesto, grind the raw and roasted cashews to a coarse powder in a food processor. Add the garlic and pulse to chop. Add the cilantro and, with the motor running, pour in the oil. Add the Parmesan and process until the mixture is creamy.

To make the stock, tie the garlic, ginger, thyme, cumin, and fennel in a piece of cheesecloth. Place the bouquet garni in a large saucepan, add the water and celery, and bring to a boil. Reduce the heat and simmer 40 minutes. Strain and set aside.

(continued from previous page)

THE SOUP

2 tablespoons olive oil

2 cloves garlic, finely chopped

1 tablespoon finely chopped gingerroot

1 medium onion, cut into 8 wedges
   and separated

2 stalks celery, cut into 1/4-inch (6-mm)
   slices

2 medium carrots, split and cut into
   1/4-inch (6-mm) slices

1 tablespoon ground cumin

1/2 tablespoon ground coriander

1 large potato, cut into 1/4-inch
   (6-mm) dice

8 ounces (230 g) green beans, cut into
   1-inch (2.5-cm) pieces

6 cups (1.5 l) boiling water

2 cups (450 g) canned cannellini beans
   or flageolets, drained

1 large tomato, peeled and cut into
   1/4-inch (6-mm) dice

2 medium zucchini (courgettes), split
   and cut into 1/4-inch (6-mm) slices

Salt and pepper

To make the soup, heat the oil in a stockpot set over medium heat and sauté the garlic, ginger, onion, celery, and carrot until soft but not browned, about 5 minutes. Stir in the cumin and coriander. Add the potato, green beans, stock, and water, and bring to a boil. Reduce the heat and simmer 15 minutes. Stir in the beans, tomato, and zucchini, and season with salt and pepper. Cover and cook 10 minutes.

Just before serving, mix the pesto with 1 cup (250 ml) of the soup liquid, pour the mixture into a tureen, and add the soup, stirring to blend.

cilantro

ULUSSOISE

1 green breadfruit (about 1 pound/
450 g), cut into 2-inch (5-cm) pieces,
or 2 8-ounce (230-g) cans
2 tablespoons unsalted butter
4 medium leeks, white part only,
thinly sliced
1 medium onion, halved and thinly sliced
4 cups (1 l) chicken stock
2 cups (500 ml) soy milk
Salt and ground white pepper
Chopped chives for garnish

Ulu, or breadfruit, a staple of the tropics, is rich in vitamin C. It can usually be found, fresh or canned, wherever there is an Asian or Caribbean population, but if you cannot find it, this recipe can also be made with another tropical staple, sweet potatoes. Either way, the result will be silky, smooth, and delicious.

Yield: 4 to 6 servings

Put the breadfruit in a large saucepan, add water to cover, and boil until soft. Drain and set aside to cool.

Melt the butter in a large sauté pan set over medium heat and sauté the leek and onion until translucent and soft, about 10 minutes. Stir in the breadfruit and stock. Reduce the heat, cover, and simmer 30 minutes.

Strain, setting aside the liquid and transferring the solids to a food processor. Purée, stopping to scrape down the sides of the bowl as necessary.

Stir the purée and soy milk into the liquid, and season with salt and pepper. Refrigerate until chilled. Sprinkle with chives just before serving.

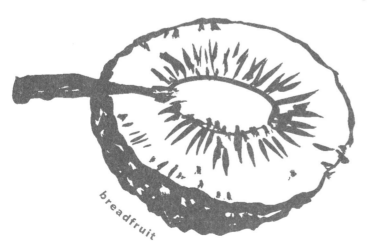

breadfruit

SWEET POTATO AND PEAR BISQUE

1½ pounds (675 g) sweet potatoes, peeled
    and cut into ½-inch (1.3-cm) chunks
2 cups (500 ml) dry white wine
¼ cup (60 ml) lemon juice
3-inch (7.5-cm) cinnamon stick
2 pears, peeled, halved, and cored
1 tablespoon unsalted butter
½ medium onion, chopped
4-inch (10-cm) piece celery, chopped
4-inch (10-cm) piece carrot, chopped
1 cup (250 ml) chicken stock
2 cups (500 ml) heavy (double) cream
¼ cup (60 ml) freshly squeezed lime juice
Salt and ground black pepper
Lime slices for garnish

I created this soup specifically with Christmas in mind. Wanting to incorporate a tropical flavor with traditional holiday fare, I decided upon sweet potatoes for a base, as they are a standard at Western holiday meals and are eaten extensively throughout the islands. To counteract the sweetness of the tuber and add a tropical touch, I blended in some lime juice. A silky pear purée adds an elegant smoothness. This soup can be served either hot or cold.

Yield: 6 to 8 servings

Put the sweet potatoes in a large saucepan, add water to cover, and boil until soft, about 30 minutes. Drain, reserving 1 cup (250 ml) of the cooking liquid, and set aside.

Put the wine, lemon juice, and cinnamon in a medium non-reactive saucepan. Add the pears and poach until tender, about 20 minutes. Drain, reserving the cooking liquid, and remove and discard the cinnamon.

Melt the butter in a large sauté pan set over medium heat and sauté the onion, celery, and carrot until soft, about 15 minutes. Transfer to a food processor, add the pears and sweet potatoes, and process until smooth. With the motor running, add the reserved pear-poaching liquid. Transfer the purée to a large saucepan and stir in the chicken stock, the reserved 1 cup (250 ml) potato-cooking liquid, and the cream.

Add the lime juice and season with salt and pepper.

To serve hot, simmer until heated through. To serve cold, refrigerate until chilled. Garnish with lime slices.

Note: For a lighter version, substitute milk or soy milk for the cream.

HAWAIIAN SEAFOOD SOUP

2 tablespoons olive oil
2 medium onions, coarsely chopped
2-inch (5-cm) piece gingerroot, finely
    chopped
3 cloves garlic, finely chopped
2 jalapeño peppers, seeded and finely
    chopped
16-ounce (450-g) can plum (egg)
    tomatoes, drained and coarsely
    chopped, canning liquid reserved
2 tablespoons freshly squeezed lemon
    juice
1½ tablespoons paprika
⅔ cup (160 ml) coconut milk
½ cup (45 g) macadamia nuts, finely
    ground
½ cup (20 g) loosely packed cilantro
    (fresh coriander), finely chopped
2 cups (500 ml) chicken stock
Salt and ground black pepper
½ pound (230 g) medium shrimp,
    peeled and deveined
½ pound (230 g) medium sea scallops
½ pound (230 g) firm fish, such as
    tuna, snapper, or swordfish, cut into
    ½-inch (1.3-cm) dice
Cilantro leaves for garnish

This variation of the popular Brazilian soup vatapá, traditionally made with dried shrimp, peanuts, and the reddish-orange high-saturated-fat palm oil called dende, substitutes fresh seafood, paprika for color, and ground macadamia nuts to thicken the soup and give it a truly Hawaiian flavor.

Yield: 4 to 6 servings

Heat the oil in a large, heavy saucepan set over low heat and cook the onions 15 minutes. Add the ginger, garlic, jalapeño, half the tomatoes, the canning liquid, the lemon juice, and the paprika. Cook 2 minutes, then add the coconut milk, ground nuts, and half the cilantro.

Transfer the soup to a food processor and purée. With the motor running, add the stock.

Return the soup to the saucepan, add the remaining tomatoes and cilantro, and bring to a boil. Season with salt and pepper, and remove from the heat. Add the shrimp, scallops, and fish, cover, and let sit 5 minutes; be careful not to overcook. Garnish with cilantro leaves and serve immediately.

HOT-AND-SOUR SHRIMP SOUP

10 dried cloud ear or other Asian
    mushrooms
1 medium carrot
1 medium leek, washed and trimmed of
    all but 2 inches (5 cm) of green
2 inches (5 cm) gingerroot
4 cups (1 l) chicken stock
2 tablespoons mirin
2 tablespoons rice vinegar
2 tablespoons white vinegar
2 tablespoons soy sauce
1 tablespoon Asian sesame oil
1 teaspoon ground black pepper
3 scallions, thinly sliced
1 stalk lemon grass, cut into 2-inch
    (5-cm) pieces, or zest of 1/2 lemon
2 tablespoons cornstarch (cornflour)
    mixed with 2 tablespoons water
1/2 pound (230 g) medium shrimp
    (prawns), peeled, deveined, and split
1/2 teaspoon hot-pepper flakes
2 eggs, beaten well

Shrimp, ginger, and lemon grass elevate the characteristic peppery-sour flavor of this soup above the ordinary. By adjusting the hot-pepper flakes and vinegar, you can control the degree of spiciness to suit individual tastes.

Yield: 4 servings

Soak the mushrooms in 2 cups (500 ml) hot water until spongy, about 30 minutes. Drain, remove and discard the stems, and thinly slice.

Peel the carrot, slice it thin on the diagonal, stack the slices, and cut them into matchsticks. Cut the leek into 2-inch (5-cm) sections and cut into matchsticks. Grate the ginger and squeeze out the juice, discarding the ginger.

Bring the stock to a boil in a large pot. Add the ginger juice, mirin, rice vinegar, white vinegar, soy sauce, oil, and black pepper. Add the carrot, scallion, leek, and lemon grass, and bring back to a low boil. Remove 1 cup (250 ml) of soup from the pot and stir it into the cornstarch slurry. Pour the mixture back into the pot, stirring. Add the shrimp and the mushrooms. Add the hot-pepper flakes and adjust seasoning.

Turn off the heat and pour the beaten eggs in a thin stream around the edge of the pot, stirring to form ribbons as the egg cooks. Serve immediately.

lemon grass

MAUI ONION SOUP WITH GOAT CHEESE TOASTS

4 tablespoons (½ stick) (55 g) unsalted
    butter
1½ pounds (675 g) Maui or Vidalia
    (sweet) onions, thinly sliced
4 large cloves garlic, thinly sliced
2 teaspoons ground fennel
2 teaspoons ground coriander
½ cup (120 ml) dry white wine
2 tablespoons mirin
4 cups (1 l) chicken stock
Salt
8 slices ½-inch- (1.3-cm-) thick
    French bread
2 ounces (55 g) creamy goat cheese
    (chèvre)

This light, aromatic version of classic French onion soup replaces the usual Gruyère with goat cheese. In Hawaii, a wonderful creamy goat cheese is produced in the Puna rain forest region of the Big Island, but any creamy goat cheese will do well. Maui onions are mild and sweet; Vidalia onions can be substituted. The onions need long cooking to allow the flavor to develop, but do not let them burn, or they will become inedible.

Yield: 4 servings

Melt the butter in a large pan set over low heat. Add the onion and cook 30 minutes, stirring frequently. Raise the heat to high and add the garlic, fennel, and coriander. Cook, stirring, 2 minutes. Add the wine and mirin, and cook, stirring, until the liquid is greatly reduced, about 3 minutes. Add the stock, bring to a boil, cover, reduce the heat to low, and simmer 20 minutes. Season with salt.

Preheat the broiler (griller). Lightly toast the bread on both sides. Remove the bread from the broiler, keeping the broiler on. When the bread has cooled slightly, spread each slice with goat cheese.

Pour the soup into heatproof bowls, float 2 toasts in each bowl, and broil until the cheese is golden, 2 or 3 minutes. Serve immediately.

PACIFIC BOUILLABAISSE

3 cups (750 ml) cold water

2 cups (500 ml) clam juice

1 cup (250 ml) dry white wine

Juice of 2 limes

1 medium onion, peeled and cut into
8 wedges

4 cloves garlic, thinly sliced

2-inch (5-cm) piece gingerroot,
thinly sliced

1/2 teaspoon red-pepper flakes

3 bay leaves

1/2 teaspoon salt

1/4 teaspoon ground black pepper

1/2 pound (230 g) medium shrimp
(prawns), peeled and deveined,
shells reserved

1/2 cup (120 ml) olive oil

1 Maui or Vidalia (large, sweet) onion,
thinly sliced

1 cup (115 g) julienned red, green, and
yellow bell peppers (capsicums)

1/2 cup (55 g) thinly sliced celery

2 teaspoons paprika

2 cups (450 g) canned or cooked navy
beans, drained

2 medium tomatoes, peeled, and cut into
1/4-inch (6-mm) dice

1 cup (40 g) loosely packed basil

1/2 pound (230 g) medium sea scallops

1 pound (450 g) firm fish, such as tuna,
snapper, or swordfish

1/4 cup (10 g) loosely packed cilantro
(fresh coriander)

Taking advantage of the Pacific Ocean's seafood bounty, this rich, spicy, and colorful soup makes an outstanding main course served with a simple tossed salad and crusty bread.

Yield: 4 to 6 servings

Put the water, clam juice, wine, lime juice, onion, garlic, ginger, red-pepper flakes, bay leaves, salt, pepper, and shrimp shells in a large saucepan, and bring to a boil. Reduce the heat and simmer 30 minutes. Strain, returning the liquid to the saucepan and discarding the solids.

Meanwhile, heat the oil in a medium sauté pan and sauté the onion, bell peppers, celery, and paprika until soft, about 5 minutes. Add to the liquid in the saucepan and bring to a boil. Add the beans and bring back to a boil. Add the tomatoes and basil, and bring back to a boil. Add the shrimp, scallops, and fish, and simmer 10 minutes. Add the cilantro, adjust the seasoning, and serve.

LOBSTER AND SCALLOP BISQUE WITH BASIL

1 pound (450 g) spiny lobster tails
4 cups (1 l) water
1 medium carrot
1 medium onion
3 cloves garlic, peeled and crushed
1 medium stalk celery, cut into 2-inch
    (5-cm) lengths
2 tablespoons olive oil
1 cup (250 ml) dry white wine
1/2 cup (120 ml) sweet vermouth
6 sprigs parsley
4 tablespoons (1/2 stick) (55 g) unsalted
    butter
2 tablespoons flour
1/2 cup (120 ml) plus 1 teaspoon heavy
    (double) cream
1 pound (450 g) medium sea scallops
1/2 cup (20 g) basil, cut into julienne
1 egg
2 sheets (10 × 12 inch/25.4 × 30.5 cm)
    frozen puff pastry, thawed
Coarse sea salt

This uniquely presented soup was inspired by the idea of combining soup with the delicate Chinese baked or steamed buns called manapua. Eaten throughout the islands, the buns are stuffed with either sweet or savory fillings. The challenge was how to get the soup inside the bun. I found the solution by covering individual bowls of soup with a thin layer of glazed dough, then baking them in a hot oven. The result is a terrific presentation, for as the dough bakes, it expands into a dramatic dome resembling a large baked manapua. Practical as well as spectacular, the dome holds in the flavors of the soup, which are released in an aromatic cloud as the crust is pierced.

Yield: 6 servings

Split the lobster tails and remove the meat, reserving the shells. Cut the meat into 1/2-inch (1.3-cm) dice and refrigerate until needed. Thinly slice one of the carrots and cut the other into 1/4-inch (6-mm) dice. Cut one of the onions into 8 wedges and the other into 1/4-inch (6-mm) dice.

Put the water in a medium, heavy saucepan and bring to a boil. Add the garlic, sliced carrot, onion wedges, celery, oil, wine, vermouth, parsley, and lobster shells. Bring back to a boil, then lower the heat and simmer 30 minutes. Strain, discarding the solids.

Heat 2 tablespoons of the butter in a small sauté pan set over medium heat and sauté the diced onion 2 minutes. Add the diced carrot and cook until soft, stirring. Remove from the heat and set aside.

Melt the remaining 2 tablespoons butter in a large saucepan

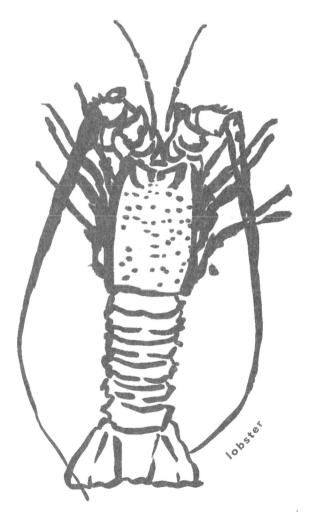

lobster

set over medium heat and stir in the flour. Continue stirring until all the butter has been absorbed. Add the strained stock a cup at a time, stirring, and cook 5 minutes. Pour in the ½ cup (120 ml) cream slowly, stirring. Turn off the heat and keep warm.

Put the sautéed carrot and onion in the food processor, pulse a few times, then process until smooth. With the motor running, pour in the soup. Add half the lobster meat and half the scallops, and process until smooth, about 30 seconds. Stir in the remaining lobster and scallops. Divide the soup among 6 4-inch- (10-cm) diameter 1-cup (250-ml) ovenproof bowls. Refrigerate until cool.

Whisk together the egg and the 1 teaspoon cream.

Unfold the puff pastry and cut out 6 5-inch (13-cm) rounds. Lightly brush the top of each round with the egg wash, reserving the remaining egg wash.

Place a pastry round over each bowl, pressing the overhang against the outside of the bowl. Be careful not to stretch or tear the dough. Place the bowls on a baking sheet and put it in the freezer. Chill 30 minutes, or until the pastry is very cold.

Preheat the oven to 400°F (200°C). Lightly brush the top of the pastry rounds with egg wash and sprinkle with salt. Place the cookie sheet with the bowls in the center of the oven and bake 10 minutes, or until the pastry has puffed into a dome. Lower the heat to 375°F (190°C) and bake 10 minutes more, or until golden brown. Serve immediately.

SALADS

The salads here combine ingredients that are both familiar and exotic, utilizing foods such as noodles, lentils, tropical fruit, and tofu, among others. In the Thai-inspired Pacific Paradise Salad (page 83), crisp shredded papaya is coated with red-pepper flakes and tossed in lime juice.

This is a terrific salad to accompany a soup served at lunch, such as Pacific Bouillabaisse (page 77), and it nicely complements Evil Jungle Prince (page 162) or Chicken Satay Pizza (page 103).

For dieters or for a salad that precedes a substantial main course, Pineapple, Jícama, and Tofu Salad (page 84) is an excellent choice—perfect served with Eggplant in Cinnamon-Chili Sauce (page 166). The refreshing sweet-acidic flavor of both dishes is due to the addition of tamarind, gentle and zesty at the same time. This salad also goes well with grilled shrimp. Another unusual salad combination that works especially well with grilled seafood is the simple-to-prepare Banana, Lentil, and Rosemary Salad (page 85).

For a change from cold salads one of my favorite meals is Spinach and Shiitake Mushroom Salad (page 86). This salad works well as an appetizer and also makes a lovely lunch dish with the addition of seared scallops or tossed in lightly sautéed garlic shrimp just before serving.

My version of a raw fish salad, Marinated Seafood Salad (page 87), is similar to the Tahitian recipe for *poisson cru*, which includes coconut milk. Other favorite salads of mine are those that combine vegetables and nuts. An exceptionally delicious way to serve broccoli is Five-Spice Broccoli Salad (page 88). Tangy Eggplant, Tomato, and Chickpea Salad (page 89) can be served as an appetizer or spread on thin toasts.

With the greater availability of exotic ingredients, try your own experiments with jícama, tamarind, soba, daikon, and all the other new salad tastes your palate is waiting to discover.

PACIFIC PARADISE SALAD

3 cloves garlic, peeled
2 teaspoons red-pepper flakes
1/4 cup (60 ml) freshly squeezed lime
   juice
1/2 teaspoon salt
1/2 teaspoon ground black pepper
1/2 cup (120 ml) vegetable oil
1 small head romaine (cos) lettuce, cut
   into bite-size pieces
2 cups (75 g) watercress, trimmed
1/2 pound (230 g) green papaya
   (pawpaw), peeled, seeded, and grated
2 tomatoes, cut into small wedges
1 avocado, halved and sliced
1 English (hothouse) cucumber, split
   and sliced 1/4-inch- (6-mm) thick on
   the diagonal

Shredded green papaya salad is a very popular item in Thailand. Generally served with a fresh lime and chili dressing, it is a great accompaniment to curried dishes. In this variation I have added some ingredients to turn a simple salad into a refreshing lunch. Green papayas can be found in Asian and Hispanic markets.

Yield: 4 servings

Drop the garlic and red-pepper flakes into a food processor or blender with the motor running. Add the lime juice, salt, and pepper, and process to blend. With the motor running, pour in the oil in a steady stream and process until well blended. Adjust the seasoning.

Toss the lettuce with the watercress and divide among 4 salad plates. Place a mound of grated papaya in the center of each plate. Arrange the tomato wedges, avocado slices, and cucumber slices attractively on the salad. Pour dressing over the top and serve.

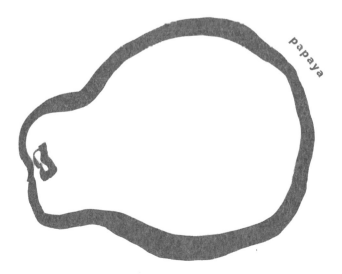

papaya

PINEAPPLE, JÍCAMA, AND TOFU SALAD

2 tablespoons tamarind paste

1/2 cup (120 ml) hot water

2 tablespoons firmly packed light-brown
   sugar

3 tablespoons roasted peanuts
   (groundnuts)

1 teaspoon red-pepper flakes

1 teaspoon salt

1/2 pineapple, peeled, cored, and cut into
   1/2-inch (1.3-cm) cubes

1 medium jícama, peeled and cut into
   julienne

1 Granny Smith (tart) apple, peeled and
   cut into 1/2-inch (1.3-cm) cubes

8 ounces (230 g) bean sprouts

4 ounces (115 g) firm tofu (soybean
   curd), cut into 1/2-inch (1.3-cm)
   cubes

This is a terrific salad for dieters. The addition of tofu makes it a light yet protein-packed meal. The dressing can be made well in advance and refrigerated.

Yield: 4 to 6 servings

Soak the tamarind paste in the water for 30 minutes. Strain the mixture, pressing the juice from the pulp; discard the pulp and put the liquid in a food processor or blender. Add the sugar, peanuts, red-pepper flakes, and salt, and process 20 seconds, or until smooth.

   Put the pineapple, jícama, apple, bean sprouts, and tofu in a large bowl. Add the dressing and toss gently. Let sit about 15 minutes before serving.

pineapple

BANANA, LENTIL, AND ROSEMARY SALAD

1 tablespoon olive oil
½ medium red onion, cut into ¼-inch
    (6-mm) dice
2 cloves garlic, finely chopped
1 red bell pepper (capsicum), cut into
    ¼-inch (6-mm) dice
1 tablespoon finely chopped rosemary
1½ cups (340 g) cold cooked brown
    lentils
2 ripe but firm bananas, cut into ¼-inch
    (6-mm) dice
¼ cup (60 ml) balsamic vinegar
Salt and ground black pepper

This unusual salad can be prepared up to 1 day ahead. It goes especially well with grilled fish or other seafood kebabs that have been marinated in lemon or lime.

Yield: 4 to 6 servings

Heat the oil in a medium sauté pan and sauté the onion and garlic until soft. Add the red pepper and rosemary, and cook 3 more minutes.

    Put the lentils and bananas in a large bowl. Add the onion mixture and vinegar, season with salt and pepper, and toss gently to mix well. Refrigerate until chilled.

ORANGE-MACADAMIA SALAD

3 oranges, preferably blood oranges
4-inch (10-cm) piece daikon, peeled and
    cut into ¼-inch (6-mm) slices
1 small head romaine (cos) lettuce,
    torn into bite-size pieces
1 bunch watercress, stems removed
¼ cup (30 g) macadamia nuts, coarsely
    chopped
¼ cup (10 g) mint, chopped
Citrus Dressing (page 99)

Light and refreshing, this salad makes a great summer lunch with soup and bread.

Yield: 6 servings

Peel the oranges with a knife, cutting away the white pith to reveal the flesh. Remove each section by cutting it away from its surrounding membranes. Cut the daikon slices into quarters. Combine the orange, daikon, lettuce, watercress, nuts, and mint in a large bowl. Add the Citrus Dressing and toss to coat.

SPINACH AND SHIITAKE MUSHROOM SALAD

*2 cups (75 g) tightly packed spinach
leaves
8 ounces (230 g) shiitake mushrooms,
cut into 1/2-inch (1.3-cm) strips
1/2 cup (55 g) grated Parmesan cheese
1/2 cup (120 ml) Balsamic Honey Dijon
Dressing (page 98)
1/2 cup (55 g) pine nuts (pine kernels),
lightly toasted*

This terrific wilted-spinach salad goes well with grilled scallops or shrimp—or combine it with a light summer soup for a special lunch.

Yield: 4 servings

Divide half the spinach among 4 salad plates and arrange half the mushrooms over it. Sprinkle half the Parmesan on top of the mushrooms and half the dressing on top of that.

Repeat the process with the remaining spinach, mushrooms, cheese, and dressing.

To toast pine nuts, heat a small frying pan over high heat. Add pine nuts and stir for about 1 minute until lightly browned. Remove from heat immediately, as nuts can easily burn.

Top salad with the pine nuts.

Just before serving, microwave at full power 30 seconds, or place in a preheated 400°F (200°C) oven for 2 minutes, or just until the spinach wilts. Serve immediately.

shiitake mushrooms

MARINATED SEAFOOD SALAD

3 cloves garlic, thinly sliced
1 medium Maui or Vidalia (sweet)
   onion, quartered
1/2 cup (20 g) basil
1/3 cup (15 g) cilantro (fresh coriander)
Zest of 1 lemon, cut into julienne
Zest of 1/2 lime, cut into julienne
1 large tomato, peeled, seeded, and cut
   into 1/4-inch (6-mm) dice
1/4 pound (115 g) sea scallops
1/4 pound (115 g) salmon, cut into
   1/4-inch (6-mm) dice
1/4 pound (115 g) mahimahi, cut into
   1/4-inch (6-mm) dice
1/4 cup (60 ml) freshly squeezed lemon
   juice
1/4 cup (60 ml) freshly squeezed lime
   juice
8 green peppercorns, crushed
Salt and ground black pepper
1 cup (250 ml) coconut milk

This delicate variation of seviche can be served as an appetizer in a radicchio leaf cup or in larger portions for a lunch.

Yield: 4 servings as an entrée, 12 as an appetizer

Drop the garlic, onion, basil, and cilantro in a food processor with the motor running, and process until finely chopped. Transfer to a large, nonreactive bowl. Blanch the lemon and lime zests by putting them in a strainer and plunging it into boiling water for 1 minute. Refresh in cold water and drain.

Add the blanched zest, tomato, scallops, salmon, mahimahi, lemon juice, lime juice, and green peppercorns to the bowl, season with salt and pepper, and toss gently. Cover and allow to marinate in the refrigerator overnight, or until the fish turns firm and opaque, tossing occasionally. Drain, add the coconut milk, and toss gently.

FIVE-SPICE BROCCOLI SALAD

1 pound (450 g) broccoli florets

5 cloves garlic, peeled

1 tablespoon soy sauce

2 teaspoons honey

1 teaspoon grated gingerroot

1 teaspoon Chinese five-spice powder

½ teaspoon ground black pepper

2 tablespoons macadamia nut oil or
    walnut oil

1 tablespoon Asian sesame oil

1 large carrot, cut into julienne

4-inch (10-cm) piece daikon, peeled and
    cut into strips with a vegetable peeler

4 scallions, thinly sliced on the diagonal

½ cup (25 g) coconut, toasted

¼ cup (30 g) coarsely chopped
    macadamia nuts

Five-spice powder is a blend of cloves, cinnamon, fennel, star anise, and ginger widely used in Chinese cooking. This is an exceptionally delicious way to serve broccoli.

Yield: 4 servings

Steam the broccoli with 3 of the garlic cloves for about 5 minutes, or until just tender.

Drop the remaining 2 cloves garlic in a food processor or blender with the motor running. Add the soy sauce, honey, ginger, five-spice powder, and pepper. With the motor still running, add the nut oil and sesame oil, and process until blended. Pour the dressing over the warm broccoli and toss to coat. Let cool completely. Remove the 3 whole cloves garlic and discard. Add the carrot, daikon, and scallion, and toss. Divide among 4 salad plates and sprinkle with the coconut and macadamia nuts.

EGGPLANT, TOMATO, AND CHICKPEA SALAD

Olive oil for sautéing

2 pounds (900 g) Japanese eggplant
   (aubergines), cut into ¼-inch
   (6-mm) rounds

1 pound (450 g) tomatoes, peeled, seeded,
   and cut into ¼-inch (6-mm) dice

3 cloves garlic, peeled and thinly sliced

1 teaspoon ground cumin

1 teaspoon paprika

¼ teaspoon cayenne

1 cup (230 g) cooked or canned
   chickpeas

1 green bell pepper (capsicum), cut into
   ¼-inch (6-mm) dice

1 red bell pepper (capsicum), cut into
   ¼-inch (6-mm) dice

¼ cup (60 ml) freshly squeezed
   lemon juice

This salad also makes a great appetizer served on thin French bread toasts.

Yield: 6 servings

Working in batches, heat some oil in a large, heavy sauté pan set over medium-high heat and sauté the eggplant until golden on both sides. Remove from the pan with a slotted spatula and drain on paper towels (kitchen paper).

Put the tomato, garlic, cumin, paprika, cayenne, chickpeas, green pepper, and red pepper in the pan and sauté until the peppers are just soft and the mixture is heated through, about 4 minutes. Transfer the mixture to a large bowl, add the eggplant and lemon juice, and toss gently. Serve at room temperature.

japanese eggplant

SESAME SOBA SALAD

8 ounces (230 g) broccoli florets
8 ounces (230 g) soba noodles (page 29)
1/4 cup (60 ml) vegetable oil
2 cups (75 g) shredded romaine (cos)
    lettuce
2 cups (160 g) bean sprouts
1 cup (80 g) thinly sliced white
    mushrooms
1/4 pound (115 g) shiitake mushrooms,
    cut into 1/4-inch (6-mm) strips
2 red bell peppers (capsicums), seeded
    and cut in thin slices
Sesame Soy Dressing (page 97)

Another of the many foods introduced to the islands by the Japanese, soba noodles are popular served both as a cold salad and in a light hot broth. If you are making this salad ahead, keep the noodles, vegetables, and dressing separately in the refrigerator, and combine at the last moment.

Yield: 4 to 6 servings

Steam the broccoli for about 5 minutes, or until just tender. Cook the noodles in lightly salted rapidly boiling water until they are al dente. Drain in a colander and rinse under cold water. Transfer to a large bowl, add the oil, and toss to coat. Add the lettuce, bean sprouts, white mushrooms, shiitake mushrooms, red pepper, and broccoli, and toss to mix. Add the dressing and toss to coat. Serve immediately.

SNOWPEA AND SHIITAKE SALAD

¹/₂ pound (230 g) snowpeas, strings removed
¹/₄ pound (115 g) shiitake mushrooms, cut into ¹/₄-inch (6-mm) strips
1 red bell pepper (capsicum), cored, seeded, and cut into ¹/₄-inch (6-mm) rings
3 cloves garlic, peeled
¹/₃ cup (80 ml) vegetable oil
1 tablespoon Asian sesame oil
2 tablespoons mirin
1 tablespoon freshly squeezed lemon juice
¹/₂ teaspoon salt
2 tablespoons sesame seeds, lightly toasted

This simple but delicious salad can be prepared well in advance and the dressing added just before serving.

Yield: 4 to 6 servings

Blanch the snowpeas by plunging them in boiling water for 1 minute. Refresh in cold water and cut them in half on the diagonal. Put the snowpeas in a large salad bowl and add the mushrooms and red pepper.

Finely chop the garlic by dropping it into a food processor or blender with the motor running. Add the vegetable oil, sesame oil, mirin, lemon juice, and salt, and process until well blended. Pour the dressing over the salad, sprinkle with the sesame seeds, toss well, and serve.

shiitake mushrooms

SALAD DRESSINGS

A dressing can transform the simplest greens into a memorable dish. I enjoy the trend of creating salad dressings that combine fresh fruit or vegetable purées with herbs and spices, replacing most of the oil or even doing away with the oil completely.

Make dressings in large quantities and store them, tightly covered, in the refrigerator. Most will keep for quite a long time, so you will always have an array to choose from.

For Caesar salad fans who are reluctant to indulge in all the fat and calories in a traditional Caesar dressing, I offer a lighter version (page 95), which uses granulated lecithin as a binder. Available in health food stores as a liquid or as granules, lecithin stabilizes salad dressings and binds the ingredients into a smooth blend.

Another recipe that uses lecithin is my alternative to mayonnaise, which I call Soyannaise (page 98). This terrific low-fat, eggless mayonnaise can be made in large quantities and kept refrigerated. Combine it with fresh herbs to create your own creamy salad dressings, or use it on sandwiches or anywhere else you would normally use mayonnaise.

A dressing that works as well on salad greens as on fruit salad is the popular island favorite Creamy Ginger Papaya-Seed Dressing (page 96). The usual version is found in dried form or bottled in supermarkets, but my recipe calls for blended fresh vegetables, giving it a rich, substantial texture and a better flavor.

For interesting tastes that take you away from the usual oil-and-vinegar dressings, experiment with your own favorite recipes by substituting Asian ingredients. Use blends of toasted sesame oil and soy sauce, or ginger with mirin or rice vinegar instead of the more familiar wine or cider vinegars. Salad dressings are a quick, easy way to explore the flavors of the Pacific.

CAESAR DRESSING

4 cloves garlic, peeled
1/2 cup (56 g) grated Parmesan cheese
1 tablespoon granulated lecithin
    (available at health food stores)
2 teaspoons powdered mustard
2 teaspoons anchovy paste
1/2 teaspoon sugar
2 tablespoons extra-virgin olive oil
1 teaspoon Worcestershire sauce
1 tablespoon freshly squeezed
    lemon juice
1/2 cup (120 ml) water

Yield: 1 cup (240 ml)

Put the garlic cloves in a food processor or blender and pulse 5 or 6 times to chop. Add the remaining ingredients and process until smooth, about 3 minutes. Add water and continue to blend until mixture is well combined.

LEMON-THYME DRESSING

3 cloves garlic, peeled
1 tablespoon sugar
1/2 cup (120 ml) olive oil
1/4 cup (60 ml) freshly squeezed
    lemon juice
2 tablespoons thyme
Salt and pepper

Light and fragrant, this dressing goes well with summer salads.

Yield: 1 cup (240 ml)

Put all the ingredients in a blender and process until smooth.

CREAMY GINGER PAPAYA-SEED DRESSING

2 tablespoons finely chopped gingerroot

1/4 cup (30 g) chopped carrot

1/4 cup (30 g) chopped celery

1/4 cup (30 g) chopped onion

1/4 cup (60 ml) canola or sunflower-
  seed oil

1/4 cup (60 ml) cider vinegar

2 tablespoons white miso

1/2 tablespoon finely chopped oil-packed
  sun-dried tomatoes

1 1/2 teaspoons sugar

1 1/2 tablespoons freshly squeezed lime
  or lemon juice

1/2 teaspoon dried basil

1/8 teaspoon ground Szechwan
  peppercorn

Seeds of 1/4 medium papaya (pawpaw)

Flesh of 1/4 medium papaya

Papaya-seed dressing is a Hawaiian Island favorite, and each region has its own version. I love this highly fragrant version, which is refreshing on any salad of greens or fruit.

Yield: 1 1/4 cups (300 ml)

Place all the ingredients in a food processor or blender and process until smooth, about 5 minutes. This will keep, refrigerated, up to 1 week.

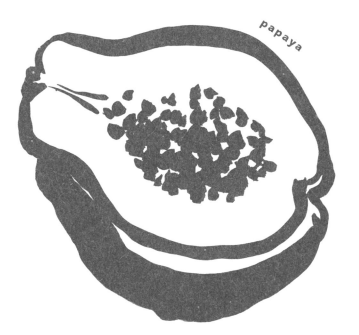

papaya

SESAME SOY DRESSING

1/4 cup (42 g) sesame seeds, toasted
1 clove garlic, chopped
2 tablespoons finely chopped gingerroot
1/2 cup (120 ml) chicken stock
1/2 cup (115 g) smooth peanut butter
1/4 cup (60 ml) red-wine vinegar
1 1/2 tablespoons soy sauce
1 1/2 tablespoons Asian sesame oil
1 tablespoon dry sherry
1 tablespoon sugar
1/4 teaspoon red-pepper flakes
1/2 teaspoon salt

This is perfect with grilled vegetables or soba noodles.

Yield: 1 1/2 cups (360 ml)

Put the sesame seeds, garlic, and ginger in a blender and process until finely chopped. Add the remaining ingredients and process until smooth.

OIL-FREE MISO DRESSING

1/4 cup (30 g) thinly sliced carrot
1/2 cup (120 ml) soy milk
2 1/2 ounces (70 g) silken tofu
　　(soybean curd)
1/4 cup (60 ml) white miso
1/4 cup (60 ml) rice vinegar
1/2 teaspoon ground ginger

This spicy, oil-free dressing is surprisingly rich and flavorful.

Yield: 1 1/4 cups (300 ml)

Steam the carrots until soft. Drain and transfer to a food processor or blender. Add the remaining ingredients and process until smooth.

BALSAMIC HONEY DIJON DRESSING

3 tablespoons Dijon mustard
$1/3$ cup (60 ml) balsamic vinegar
$1/3$ cup (60 ml) olive oil
$1^1/4$ tablespoon honey

This dressing works well on just about any salad, but I especially enjoy it with Spinach and Shiitake Mushroom Salad (page 86).

Yield: $2/3$ cup (160 ml)

Put all the ingredients in a blender and process until smooth.

SOYANNAISE

10 ounces (280 g) firm silken tofu
  (soybean curd)
2 teaspoons garlic powder
3 teaspoons granulated lecithin
  (available at health food stores)
1 teaspoon powdered mustard
1 teaspoon Dijon mustard
1 tablespoon rice vinegar
1 tablespoon freshly squeezed
  lemon juice
$1/4$ cup (60 ml) canola oil
1 teaspoon salt
$1/2$ teaspoon ground white pepper

This low-fat, eggless mayonnaise is a delicious alternative and considered by many tasters to be even better than the original.

Yield: $1^1/2$ cups (360 ml)

Put all the ingredients in a food processor or blender and process until smooth. Let sit 30 minutes before using. Keep refrigerated.

LEMON-TAHINI DRESSING

1/2 cup (225 g) tahini
1/2 cup (120 ml) water
2 tablespoons freshly squeezed
   lemon juice
1/4 teaspoon asafetida (optional)
1/2 teaspoon salt

Rich and silky smooth, this is the perfect dressing for an Asian noodle salad or served over grilled chicken with mesclun.

Yield: 1 1/4 cups (300 ml)

Put all the ingredients in a blender and process until smooth.

CITRUS DRESSING

1/4 cup (60 ml) freshly squeezed orange
   juice
2 tablespoons freshly squeezed
   lemon juice
2 teaspoons grated orange zest
1 teaspoon grated lemon zest
1/2 teaspoon ground cinnamon
1/2 teaspoon salt
1 tablespoon honey
1/4 cup (60 ml) vegetable oil

An interesting balance of tartness and sweetness, this dressing elevates any salad ingredients with its fragrant citrus flavors.

Yield: 1 cup (240 ml)

Put all dressing ingredients except the oil in a blender and process until smooth. With the motor running, pour in oil in a steady stream. Adjust the seasoning with salt.

PIZZAS AND GALETTES

In the
not-too-distant past, pizza
meant just one thing: a flat, circular piece
of dough, tomato sauce, cheese, and a more or less
unchanging selection of toppings, such as bell peppers,
onions, olives, mushrooms, and pepperoni. Not anymore.
Easy to make and easy to serve, pizzas have become an ideal
base on which to play with new cuisines. East meets West in the
rich and delicious flavors of Shiitake, Artichoke, and Gorgonzola
Pizza (page 105). Traditional mozzarella and Parmesan have been
replaced with creamy white goat cheese in the recipe for Goat
Cheese with Tricolor Pepper Pizza (page 104).
Not only have we tossed tradition to the wind by changing
the toppings, we've also changed the base. Now pizzas
are made on just about anything, from muffin halves
to filo dough. Spreading delicious ingredients on
filo makes wonderful pizzas, such as the
Parmesan Filo Pizza, with its
spinach, red

onion, and feta cheese (page 106), and the luscious Tomato-Basil Filo Pizza (page 107).

The recipes here are for 12-inch (30.5-cm) pies, but you can also use these recipes to make smaller pizzas to serve as a pupu at a party. Roll the dough into a cylinder about 3½ inches (8.9 cm) in diameter. With a sharp knife, cut the roll into ½-inch (1.3-cm) slices. Flatten the discs with a rolling pin and arrange them 1 inch (2.5 cm) apart on an oiled baking tray lightly dusted with cornmeal. If I'm preparing for a party, I'll do all this ahead of time, wrap the entire tray in plastic wrap, and place it in the freezer. When party time arrives, pop the frozen pizzas straight into a preheated 400°F (200°C) oven and bake until the crust turns a medium golden brown and the top is sizzling.

Galettes have delectable crusts that are thinner and more tender than traditional pizza crusts, and their fillings are generally more substantial. Galettes are excellent served hot or cold, with a salad course at a meal or cut into thin wedges and offered as hors d'oeuvres. Hawaiian Sweet Potato Galette with Roquefort cheese and sage (page 109) is one such sumptuous treat.

Pizzas and galettes never fail to be big hits at parties, from formal affairs to the most casual gatherings. If you keep the toppings simple, they are also great for children's parties. Try adapting a favorite recipe and making your own gourmet pizza. You never know what inspired creation you may come up with.

BASIC PIZZA DOUGH

1 package (7 g) active dry yeast
1 teaspoon sugar
1/2 cup (120 ml) warm water
1 1/2 cups (215 g) all-purpose (plain) flour
1 teaspoon salt
2 teaspoons vegetable oil

Yield: enough dough for 1 12-inch (30.5-cm) pie

Mix the yeast and sugar with the water and let stand 10 minutes. Put the flour and the salt in a food processor and process to mix. With the motor running, add the yeast mixture and oil in a steady stream. Process until incorporated and a soft dough forms, then continue processing to knead, about 40 seconds more. Add more flour 1 tablespoon at a time if the dough is too sticky.

CHICKEN SATAY PIZZA

Peanut oil
Basic Pizza Dough (page 103)
1 1/2 cups (375 ml) Peanut Satay Sauce
   (page 149)
1 pound (450 g) skinless boneless cooked
   chicken breast, cut into 1/2-inch
   (1.3-cm) dice
6 ounces (170 g) mozzarella, shredded
1 medium zucchini (courgette),
   cut into julienne
1 medium carrot, grated
1/2 cup (20 g) loosely packed cilantro
   (fresh coriander)
1 1/2 cups (85 g) bean sprouts

For a vegetarian version, substitute 12 ounces (345 g) firm tofu for the chicken.

Yield: 1 12-inch (30.5-cm) pie

Preheat the oven to 450°F (230°C) and lightly oil a baking sheet or pizza pan.

Roll the dough out on a floured surface and place it on the prepared pan. Spread with the satay sauce. Arrange the chicken evenly over the sauce. Sprinkle with half the mozzarella, then the zucchini, carrot, and cilantro. Top with the rest of the mozzarella and brush with oil. Bake 25 minutes, or until the crust is golden and the filling is bubbling. Top with bean sprouts and serve.

GOAT CHEESE WITH TRICOLOR PEPPER PIZZA

Yield: 1 12-inch (30.5-cm) pie

Olive oil
Basic Pizza Dough (page 103)
Red Pepper and Macadamia Nut Pesto
  (page 197)
1 pound (450 g) plum (egg) tomatoes,
  peeled, seeded, and coarsely chopped
6 ounces (170 g) goat cheese (chèvre),
  crumbled
1 each large red, yellow, and green bell
  pepper (capsicum), cut into 1/4-inch
  (6-mm) strips
1 red onion, peeled and cut into
  8 wedges and separated
1/2 cup (20 g) basil, cut into strips

Preheat the oven to 375°F (190°C) and lightly oil a baking sheet or pizza pan. Roll the dough out on a floured surface and place it on the prepared pan. Spread with the pesto. Arrange the tomato evenly over the pesto. Sprinkle the crumbled cheese on top. Arrange the pepper strips and onion pieces attractively on the pie. Sprinkle with basil and brush with olive oil. Bake 20 minutes, or until the crust is golden brown and the filling is bubbling.

bell pepper

SHIITAKE, ARTICHOKE, AND GORGONZOLA PIZZA

Vegetable oil for greasing pan
3 cloves garlic, finely chopped
1 cup (115 g) crumbled Gorgonzola
  cheese (about 4 ounces)
1/2 cup (120 ml) sour cream
3 tablespoons finely chopped rosemary
2 teaspoons salt
1 teaspoon ground black pepper
Basic Pizza Dough (page 103)
1 pound (450 g) shiitake mushrooms,
  cut into 1/2-inch (1.3-cm) strips
1 pound (450 g) artichoke hearts packed
  in oil, well drained
1/4 cup (10 g) chopped flat-leaf parsley
1/2 cup (55 g) grated Parmesan cheese

This rich and flavorful pizza is one of my favorites.

Yield: 1 12-inch (30.5-cm) pie

Preheat the oven to 375°F (190°C) and lightly oil a baking sheet or pizza pan.

Put the garlic, Gorgonzola, sour cream, rosemary, salt, and pepper in a food processor. Pulse 3 times, then process about 5 seconds to combine. The mixture should be well blended but slightly lumpy.

Roll the dough out on a floured surface and place it on the prepared pan.

Spread with the Gorgonzola mixture and arrange the mushrooms and artichoke hearts attractively on top. Sprinkle with the parsley and Parmesan. Bake about 25 minutes, or until the crust is nicely browned and the filling is bubbling.

PARMESAN FILO PIZZA WITH SPINACH

1/2 cup sun-dried tomatoes

1 1/2 pounds (675 g) spinach, washed
  and trimmed

8 tablespoons (1 stick) (115 g) unsalted
  butter, melted

8 14 × 14-inch (35.5 × 35.5-cm) sheets
  frozen filo dough, thawed

1/2 cup (55 g) grated Parmesan cheese

1 medium red onion, very thinly sliced

1 cup (120 g) kalamata olives, coarsely
  chopped

1 tablespoon ground cumin

2 tablespoons marjoram

1 cup (115 g) crumbled feta cheese

1/4 cup (60 ml) olive oil

Filo pizzas are a fun alternative to regular dough pizzas. I keep a package of filo dough handy in the freezer and try out a variety of toppings to serve guests. Here are some of my favorites.

Yield: 6 to 8 servings as a pupu

Soak the tomatoes in warm water 30 minutes. Drain and cut into 1/4-inch (6-mm) slices.

Preheat the oven to 400°F (200°C).

Steam the spinach 3 minutes, or until just wilted. Transfer to a colander and rinse under cold water. Squeeze as much moisture as possible from the spinach, and set aside.

Brush a baking sheet with melted butter and cover it with 1 sheet of the filo. Brush the dough lightly with butter and sprinkle with 1 tablespoon of the Parmesan.

Place another sheet of filo on top, and repeat the procedure until the last sheet is placed on top of the stack. Tamp down gently with your palms so all the sheets adhere. Brush the last layer with butter.

Bake 5 minutes, then sprinkle with the remaining Parmesan and spread the spinach evenly over it. Top with the onion, olives, and tomatoes. Sprinkle with the cumin and marjoram. Top with the feta and drizzle with the olive oil. Bake until the cheese is melted, about 15 minutes. Cut into squares with a sharp knife or a pizza wheel.

TOMATO-BASIL FILO PIZZA

Yield: 6 to 8 servings as a pupu

8 tablespoons (1 stick) (115 g) unsalted
   butter, melted
8 14 × 14-inch (35.5 × 35.5-cm) sheets
   frozen filo dough, thawed
1/2 cup (55 g) grated Parmesan cheese
1 cup (115 g) shredded mozzarella
1 cup (115 g) thinly sliced Maui or
   Vidalia (sweet) onion
2 pounds (900 g) plum (egg) tomatoes,
   sliced 1/4-inch (6-mm) thick
1/2 cup (20 g) shredded basil
1/4 cup (60 ml) extra-virgin olive oil
1 tablespoon freshly squeezed lime juice
1/2 cup (55 g) pine nuts (pine kernels)
Salt and coarsely ground black pepper
Papaya-Mango-Mint Salsa (page 188)

Preheat the oven to 400°F (200°C) and brush a baking sheet lightly with butter. Cover with 1 sheet of the filo and brush lightly with butter. Sprinkle 1 tablespoon of the Parmesan over the top. Cover with another sheet of filo, and continue the procedure until the last sheet is placed on top of the stack. Brush with butter and bake 5 minutes. Sprinkle with the remaining Parmesan and half the mozzarella. Top with the sliced onion, and arrange the tomato slices on top in a single layer. Sprinkle with remaining mozzarella and the basil.

Combine the olive oil and lime juice and brush the mixture on top of the pie. Sprinkle with the pine nuts, season with salt and pepper, and bake about 25 minutes, or until the crust is golden.

Cut into squares with a sharp knife and spoon a little of the salsa on top of each slice.

GALETTE PASTRY

1½ cups (215 g) all-purpose (plain) flour
½ teaspoon salt
8 tablespoons (1 stick) (115 g) cold
   unsalted butter, cut into 8 pieces
¼ cup (60 ml) cold water

With a thinner, more tender crust than pizzas and more substantial fillings, galettes are an excellent meal in themselves served hot or at room temperature. Cut it in pieces for a pupu or eat it with a green salad for lunch.

Yield: 1 12-inch (30.5-cm) galette

Put the flour and salt in a food processor and pulse to mix. Add the butter, pulse 4 times, then process until the mixture resembles bread crumbs. With the motor running, add water until the dough just holds together.

On a floured surface, knead the dough into a smooth ball. Flatten into a disc, cover with plastic wrap (cling film), and refrigerate at least 30 minutes.

HAWAIIAN SWEET POTATO GALETTE

Vegetable oil for greasing pan
Galette Pastry (page 108)
2½ pounds (1.1 kg) sweet potatoes,
    peeled and cut into 1-inch
    (2.5-cm) cubes
3 tablespoons olive oil
4 cloves garlic, finely chopped
1 medium onion, finely chopped
½ cup (20 g) loosely packed sage,
    coarsely chopped
1 teaspoon salt
1 teaspoon ground black pepper
½ cup (55 g) grated Romano cheese
1 cup (115 g) crumbled Roquefort
    cheese
1 egg, beaten lightly

Yield: 4 servings as an entrée, 10 as a pupu

Preheat the oven to 400°F (200°C) and lightly oil a baking sheet. Roll the dough into a 14-inch (35.5-cm) circle and place it on the sheet.

Steam the sweet potatoes until tender, about 15 minutes. Drain and set aside to cool.

Meanwhile, heat the olive oil in a small sauté pan set over medium heat and sauté the garlic, onion, and sage until soft, about 5 minutes. Add the salt and pepper, and transfer the mixture to a food processor. Add the cooked sweet potatoes and pulse 5 times. Add the Romano cheese and process until blended but still chunky, about 5 seconds. Add the Roquefort and pulse 4 times to incorporate; do not let the mixture get too smooth.

Spread the filling over the pastry, leaving a 2-inch (5-cm) border. Fold the border in over the filling, pleating and crimping it. Brush the exposed dough with beaten egg and bake until the filling is hot and the crust golden brown, about 30 minutes. Cut into wedges and serve warm or at room temperature.

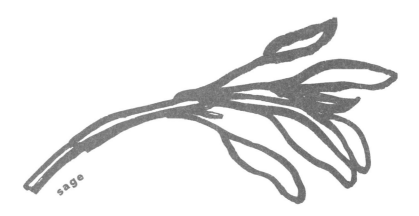

sage

MUSHROOM AND CELERIAC GALETTE

Vegetable oil for greasing pan
Galette Pastry (page 108)
3 tablespoons olive oil
1 medium onion, finely chopped
4 cloves garlic, finely chopped
1 small celeriac
Juice of 1 lemon
1 tablespoon finely chopped tarragon
1/2 pound (230 g) small white
   mushrooms, cut into 1/2-inch
   (1.3-cm) slices
1/2 pound (230 g) shiitake mushrooms,
   cut into 1/2-inch (1.3-cm) slices
1/4 pound (115 g) oyster mushrooms,
   cut into 1/2-inch (1.3-cm) slices
Salt and ground black pepper
1/2 cup (120 ml) sour cream
2 tablespoons grated Parmesan cheese
1/2 cup (20 g) finely chopped flat-leaf
   parsley
1 large egg, lightly beaten

Yield: 4 servings as an entrée, 10 as a pupu

Preheat the oven to 400°F (200°C) and lightly oil a baking sheet. Roll the dough into a 14-inch (35.5-cm) circle and place it on the baking sheet.

Heat the olive oil in a large sauté pan set over medium-low heat, and sauté the onion and garlic until soft, about 5 minutes. Meanwhile, peel the celeriac and grate it. Add the grated celeriac, half the lemon juice, and the tarragon to the pan, and cook until the liquid is evaporated and the celeriac is tender. Add the white, shiitake, and oyster mushrooms and the remaining half of the lemon juice, and cook 2 minutes more. Season with salt and pepper. Remove from the heat and stir in the sour cream, Parmesan, and half the parsley.

Spread the filling over the pastry, leaving a 2-inch (5-cm) border. Fold the border in over the filling, pleating and crimping it. Brush the exposed dough with the beaten egg and bake until the filling is hot and the crust golden brown, about 30 minutes. Cut into wedges, sprinkle with the remaining parsley, and serve warm or at room temperature.

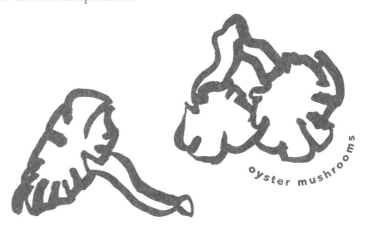

oyster mushrooms

LEAFY GREEN AND FETA GALETTE

Vegetable oil for greasing pan
Galette Pastry (page 108)
4 pounds (1.8 kg) mixed leafy greens,
    such as spinach, beet greens, Swiss
    chard, kale, arugula, and collard,
    washed and trimmed
1 tablespoon olive oil
1 medium onion, finely chopped
8 ounces (230 g) feta cheese, crumbled
4 ounces (115 g) cream cheese
1/2 cup (55 g) grated Parmesan cheese
Salt and ground black pepper
2 large eggs, lightly beaten

Yield: 4 servings as an entrée, 10 as a pupu

Preheat the oven to 400°F (200°C) and lightly oil a baking sheet. Roll the dough into a 14-inch (35.5-cm) circle and place it on the baking sheet.

Steam the greens until wilted and tender, about 3 minutes. Squeeze out as much liquid as possible. Chop fine, then squeeze to remove liquid again.

Heat the olive oil in a medium sauté pan set over medium heat, and sauté the onion until soft, about 5 minutes.

Combine the feta, cream cheese, and Parmesan in a large bowl. Add the greens and onion, season with salt and pepper, and mix well. Stir in half the beaten egg.

Spread the filling over the pastry, leaving a 2-inch (5-cm) border. Fold the border in over the filling, pleating and crimping it. Brush the exposed dough with beaten egg and bake until the filling is hot and the crust golden brown, about 30 minutes. Cut into wedges and serve warm or at room temperature.

FISH AND SEAFOOD

Surely
one of the
many joys Of
living on an island
is the availability of
so much fresh fish.
Teeming with the
widest variety
imaginable, the
Pacific Ocean's
harvest shapes
and determines
the diets of
all the
peoples
that live
along
its
shores.
With clear
waters and a
gentle breeze

the oceanfront offers simple pleasures for fishermen and spectators alike. On weekends along the rocky coastlines you can watch families set up camp just feet from the water. During the day children and adults spend their time harvesting opihi, a delectable sweet mollusk that clings fiercely to the slippery rocks. At night the hardier fishermen cast their lines off the cliffs into the seething waters. In the silvery dawn groups of young men wade out into the glistening surf and cast long nets over the reefs with a sweeping, arching curve. The thin nets settle on the water, and the men gently pull them back in a smooth motion, emptying the catch into buckets on the beach, where the children run to sort through the treasures.

A visit to the fish auction will reveal the fishermen at a less leisurely pace. At dawn the fishing boats start coming in, and the catch is rapidly unloaded and spread out on the tables. Alert, hyped-up buyers hustle back and forth, eyes darting over the gleaming fish, sharp knives slicing into a piece of flesh near the tail to assess the quality. Bidding begins immediately. The buyers represent companies from all over the world. They're moving fast because the quicker the fish is packed on ice and shipped to its destination, the more valuable the catch will be.

Tens of thousands of pounds move through the market every day. The largest percentage of the catch goes to Asia, to be served up as sashimi. Most of the remainder finds its way into huge containers, which are then shipped off to the large supermarket chains throughout the country. But enough is still left on the islands to stock the smaller fish markets that supply the local people, who consume twice as much fish per capita as anywhere else in the country.

Hawaii's reputation for good fish has suffered sadly in past years owing to the unfortunate serving of deep-fried mahimahi that is drab and soggy from being frozen, which appears on the typical tourist menu. The situation has fortunately changed with the arrival of a new breed of chefs cooking at the glamorous resorts. These five-star chefs work in harmony with local fishermen and farmers and offer a plethora of exotic produce and the most interesting fish dishes. These wonderful creations are cooked to perfection and then served up with fresh tangy salsas or marinated in exotic Asiatic spices. Other popular methods are blackened fish paired with organic mesclun and seafood crusted in crushed macadamia nuts or sesame seeds, sautéed, and garnished with fresh edible flowers grown by enterprising farmers on the fertile slopes of the volcanos.

The tantalizing choices are growing with such dishes as seafood enfolded in light wonton wrappers with a fragrant ginger sauce or baked in filo, as in Salmon in Filo with Spinach-Lime Soufflé (page 120). Fish often comes grilled and skewered with fresh tropical fruit, as in Shrimp and Papaya Skewers (page 119).

The Asian influence has introduced many new methods of preparation and lots of superb tastes with the inclusion of many herbs previously outside the experience of mainstream Western taste. A variety of cultures come into play with the selection of fish and seafood recipes here. For a variation of everyone's favorite dish from Spain, the recipe for Paella Pacifica (page 122) is a dish that truly combines Mediterranean with Eastern flavors. The quick-to-prepare Scallop and Shrimp Stir-Fry in orange sauce (page 124) is an Asian-inspired savory citrus treat. Serve the stir-fry over Pan-Fried Noodles (page 183), and discover an innovative way to use left-over noodles.

Curries are yet another way to sample and enjoy the bounty of the Pacific. The best curries are those in which the sauce is cooked first and the seafood added at the last minute, cooking just long enough to allow the fish to lose its translucence. Accompany it with a delicious chutney, such as Banana-Raisin Chutney (page 192) or Mango Chutney (page 194).

Look for Pacific fish and experiment with a familiar or favorite seafood recipe of your own by substituting a fish that is less familiar.

As a general guideline, lighter, more delicate fish are opakapaka, a pink snapper and certainly one of the favorites of island fish eaters, and onaga, a delicate red snapper. My recipe teams the sweet, tender, and juicy pink snapper with spices and coconut in Spicy Coconut Opakapaka (page 126).

Moderate-flavored fish that you may find available are kajiki (blue marlin), swordfish, uku (a gray snapper with firm flesh), and ono (a savory white flaky-textured fish also called "wahoo"). Try the aromatic Spice Island Swordfish Skewers (page 128) and Ono with Macadamia Nuts and Lime (page 129). The ubiquitous mahimahi is raised to new heights when served in tangerine sauce (page 130).

Stronger, richer-flavored fish include monchong (pomfret) and opah (also known as moonfish), a very large, brightly colored but bony fish.

And of course there is ahi, otherwise known as yellowfin tuna or bigeye, and favored for sashimi, in which the choicest cut of very fresh raw ahi is sliced thin and served with wasabi. Steaks can be quickly seared over high heat, leaving the center still uncooked, as in Sesame-Ginger-Crusted Ahi (page 131). A poorer cousin to ahi is aku, which works well in the strongly spiced Grilled Fish in Hot Tamarind Sauce (page 132). Aku is also known as skipjack tuna or oceanic bonito and has a deep red, firm flesh.

With pasta, noodles, rice, or in a steaming seafood broth or stew, the bounty of the Pacific Ocean opens a treasure chest of light, fresh, and intriguingly spiced fare.

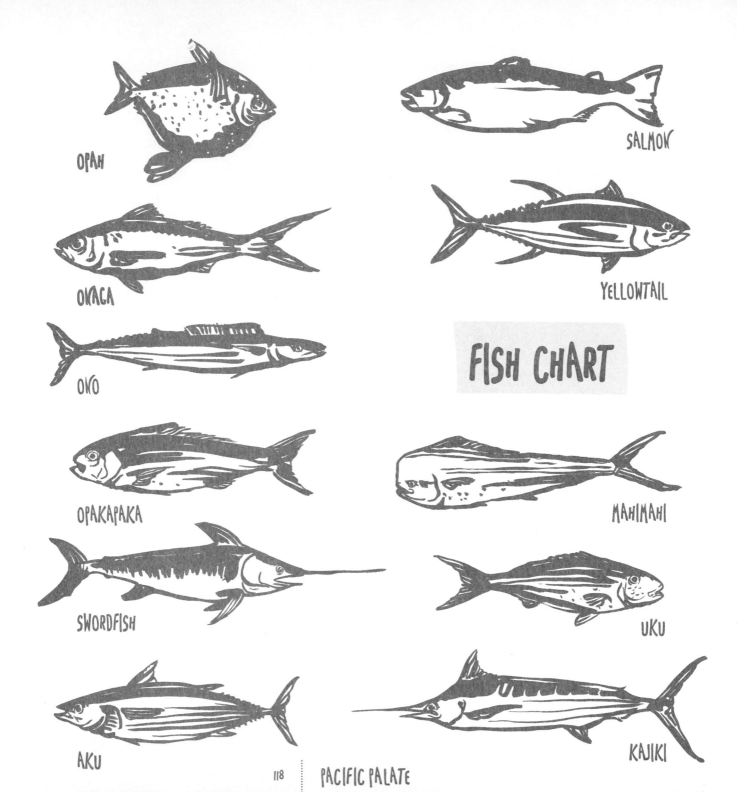

OPAH

SALMON

OKAGA

YELLOWTAIL

ONO

FISH CHART

OPAKAPAKA

MAHIMAHI

SWORDFISH

UKU

AKU

KAJIKI

SHRIMP AND PAPAYA SKEWERS

4 cloves garlic, peeled

1 jalapeño pepper, seeded

2 tablespoons vegetable oil

Juice of 1 lime

1 teaspoon paprika

1 teaspoon ground turmeric

24 large shrimp (prawns), peeled and
    deveined, tails left on

1 ripe but firm papaya (pawpaw), seeded
    and cut into 1-inch (2.5-cm) cubes

2 tablespoons chopped cilantro (fresh
    coriander)

Thin lime slices for garnish

This colorful combination works well both as an appetizer and as a first course at a dinner. Serve with Mango Chutney (page 194).

Yield: 6 servings

Chop the garlic and jalapeño by dropping them into a food processor with the motor running. Add the oil, lime juice, paprika, and turmeric, and process until well blended. Thread 6 skewers, alternating shrimp and papaya cubes. Place the skewers in one layer in a glass baking dish and add the marinade. Cover and refrigerate 30 minutes, basting occasionally.

Preheat the broiler (griller). Drain the skewers and cook 3 minutes on each side, basting with marinade. Sprinkle with the chopped cilantro and garnish with lime slices.

shrimp

SALMON IN FILO WITH SPINACH-LIME SOUFFLÉ

1 pound (450 g) chopped fresh spinach
   or 10-ounce (280 g) bag frozen,
   thawed
1 tablespoon olive oil
$^{1}/_{2}$ medium onion, finely chopped
3 cloves garlic, finely chopped
2 tablespoons freshly squeezed lime juice
Salt and ground black pepper
3 large egg whites
$^{1}/_{2}$ pound (2 sticks) (230 g) butter, melted
5 sheets filo pastry, thawed
4 teaspoons grated lime zest
2 salmon fillets, 1 pound/450 g each,
   skin removed

This stunning entrée is surprisingly simple to prepare. Topped with the easy-to-assemble filo roses and presented on a bed of fresh herbs with wild rice and steamed baby vegetables, it makes a five-star presentation. It can also be prepared ahead, baked, sliced, and served cold at a buffet.

Yield: serves 6 as an entrée, 12 as an appetizer

Preheat the oven to 400°F (200°C). If using frozen spinach, squeeze out as much moisture as possible.

Heat the oil in a medium, heavy sauté pan set over medium heat. Add the onion and garlic and cook 3 minutes, or until soft but not browned. Add the spinach and lime juice, and season with salt and pepper. Cook 3 minutes more. Allow to cool, then place in a food processor and pulse until smooth.

Beat the egg whites until stiff, and fold in the spinach mixture.

Brush a heavy baking sheet with butter. Place 1 sheet of filo on the baking sheet, brush with butter, and sprinkle with 1 teaspoon of the lime zest. Repeat with the next 3 sheets of pastry. Place one of the salmon fillets in the center of the sheet. Top with the spinach mixture, smoothing the sides and flattening the top with a spatula. Place the remaining fillet gently on top of the spinach, and brush the top of the salmon with butter.

SALMON IN FILO . . . *(continued)*

Lift the long sides of the filo and fold them on top of the salmon, tucking the short sides in, as if wrapping a package. Brush all over with butter. Cut the last filo sheet in half lengthwise. Place one of the halves on top of the pastry, tucking the sides under to hide the edges and create a smooth surface. To make filo roses, place the remaining half sheet of filo on a work surface, brush with melted butter, and, starting at the long side, fold the pastry over 1 inch (2.5 cm). Continue folding the pastry over itself, forming a 1-inch- (2.5-cm-) wide strip. Cut this into 3 pieces, and roll each strip up into a coil. Squeeze the bottom of the coil, forcing the top to open slightly and form a rose. Place each rose in a line on top of the bundle, pushing down so the roses stick to the buttered surface. Brush with any remaining butter.

Bake 35 minutes. If the roses are browning too quickly, cover loosely with foil. Remove from the oven and let sit 20 minutes before serving. Cut into 1½-inch (4-cm) slices with a serrated knife.

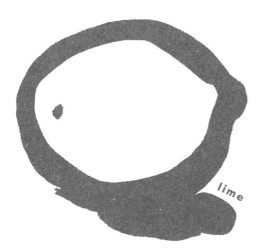

lime

PAELLA PACIFICA

2/3 cup (160 ml) olive oil

1 small chicken, hacked into 16 pieces

Salt and ground black pepper

24 large shrimp (prawns), shelled and
    deveined, tails left on, shells reserved

1 tablespoon grated gingerroot

3 red chili peppers

2 tablespoons freshly squeezed
    lemon juice

1 large onion, cut into 1/4-inch
    (6-mm) dice

6 cloves garlic, finely chopped

1 green bell pepper (capsicum), cut into
    1/4-inch (6-mm) slices

3 plum (egg) tomatoes, seeded and cut
    into 1/4-inch (6-mm) dice

2 cups (300 g) medium-grain white rice

(continued on next page)

With its combination of rice, chicken, and seafood and its colorful display of yellow saffron, red pimientos, pink shrimp, and green peas, paella is Spain's best-known culinary triumph. There are hundreds of versions of paella, with each region adjusting the combination of seafood and vegetables to its own particular bounty. I have created this Pacific Rim version by replacing the Mediterranean flavors with Pacific herbs. I have also substituted turmeric for the traditional saffron that gives Paella its golden color. If you prepare all the ingredients in advance, it is fairly simple and quick to assemble. If you don't have the traditional two-handled paella pan, use any large, shallow, heavy pan. Wash it all down with chilled dry wine, beer, or Pacific Sangría (page 18).

Yield: 8 to 10 servings

In a paella pan or any large, shallow, ovenproof pan at least 12 inches (30.5 cm) in diameter, heat 1/3 cup (80 ml) of the olive oil over medium-high heat. Season the chicken with salt and pepper and place it in the pan, skin side down. Brown well, turning regularly with tongs so the pieces color evenly without burning. Reduce the heat and continue cooking until cooked through.

While the chicken is cooking, prepare the shrimp stock by bringing to the boil the shrimp shells, ginger, chili peppers, lemon juice, and 1 teaspoon each salt and pepper in 3 cups (750 ml) of

PAELLA PACIFICA *(continued)*

(continued from previous page)

3 teaspoons ground turmeric

1/2 cup (20 g) chopped cilantro
  (fresh coriander)

1/2 cup (20 g) thinly sliced basil

1 pound (450 g) squid, cleaned and
  cut into 1/2-inch (1.3-cm) rings

1/2 pound (230 g) firm-fleshed fish, such
  as marlin, swordfish, ahi, or ono,
  cut into 3/4-inch (2-cm) cubes

16 mussels, shelled

1 red bell pepper (capsicum), peeled and
  cut into 1/2-inch (1.3-cm) strips

2 ounces (55 g) snowpeas, strings
  removed, blanched, and cut in half
  on the diagonal

2 tablespoons finely chopped parsley

Lime wedges for garnish

water. Reduce the heat and simmer 30 minutes. Strain, discarding the solids; there should be about 2 cups (500 ml) liquid.

After removing the chicken from the pan, discard all the fat and any burned pieces and add the remaining 1/3 cup (80 ml) olive oil. Heat and add the onion, garlic, green pepper, and tomato, stirring continually. Cook over medium-high heat until most of the liquid has evaporated, about 5 minutes. Add the rice and turmeric and stir to coat. Stir in the shrimp stock. Bring 3 cups (750 ml) of water to a boil and add the liquid to the paella, stirring. Cook 10 minutes, or until the rice just softens and has absorbed most of the liquid. Add salt and pepper to taste.

Reduce the heat to low and stir in the cilantro, basil, squid, and fish. Smooth the rice to make a flat surface.

Add the chicken pieces to the pan by pushing them gently into the rice. Then arrange the shrimp, mussels, red pepper strips, and snowpeas attractively on top of the rice in a circle.

Turn off the heat and cover tightly with aluminum foil. Let sit 10 minutes. Remove the cover; the shrimp should be cooked through. Sprinkle with parsley and garnish with lime wedges. Serve directly from the pan.

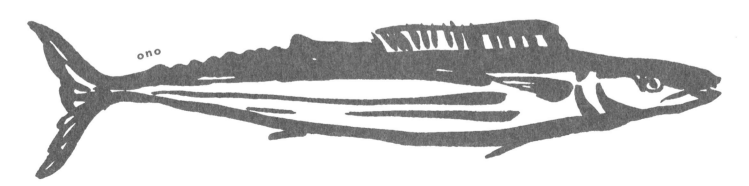

ono

SCALLOP AND SHRIMP STIR-FRY

4 tablespoons (^{1}/2 stick) (55 g) unsalted
　　butter

3 cloves garlic, finely chopped

1 large red onion, thinly sliced

1 green bell pepper (capsicum), halved
　　and thinly sliced

1 red bell pepper (capsicum), halved and
　　thinly sliced

3 tablespoons grated orange zest

2 teaspoons grated lemon zest

^{1}/4 teaspoon cayenne

^{3}/4 pound (340 g) large sea scallops

^{3}/4 pound (340 g) medium-large shrimp
　　(prawns), peeled, deveined, and split

1 teaspoon salt

1^1/2 cups (375 ml) freshly squeezed
　　orange juice

2 tablespoons freshly squeezed
　　lemon juice

^{1}/4 cup (60 ml) Cognac

4 scallions, thinly sliced

^{1}/2 cup (55 g) small peas, fresh or frozen

2 tablespoons chopped cilantro
　　(fresh coriander)

This colorful, light dish can be served at a casual supper or a summer lunch. It goes well with Pan-Fried Noodles (page 183).

Yield: 4 to 6 servings

Melt 2 tablespoons of the butter in a large sauté pan or wok set over medium heat. Add the garlic, onion, green pepper, red pepper, orange zest, lemon zest, and cayenne. Cook, stirring, 5 minutes, or until the vegetables are barely tender. Transfer to a plate.

Sprinkle the scallops and shrimp with the salt. Melt the remaining 2 tablespoons butter in the pan set over medium-high heat. Add the scallops and shrimp and stir-fry 2 minutes. Cover and cook 2 minutes more, stirring every 30 seconds, until the seafood just turns opaque. Transfer to the plate with the vegetables.

Turn the heat up to high and add the orange and lemon juice to the pan, stirring. Cook until reduced by half, 4 or 5 minutes. Stir in the Cognac, cook another minute, then add the seafood and vegetables. Stir in the scallions, peas, and cilantro and the rest of the butter. Serve immediately with quinoa or rice and a green salad.

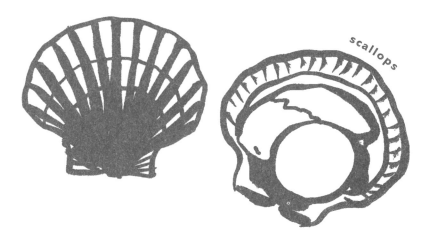

scallops

SEAFOOD CURRY

5-inch (13-cm) piece lemon grass
1½ cups (375 ml) coconut milk
½ cup (120 ml) water
1 pound (450 g) mussels
1 pound (450 g) clams
5 cloves garlic, peeled
2 medium onions, peeled and quartered
1 ounce (30 g) macadamia nuts
2 teaspoons ground cumin
2 teaspoons ground coriander
2 teaspoons curry powder
½ teaspoon red-pepper flakes
2 teaspoons salt
2 tablespoons vegetable oil
1 teaspoon rice vinegar
1 pound (450 g) medium shrimp
    (prawns), shelled and deveined
½ pound (230 g) sea scallops

Serve this aromatic seafood curry with rice and Banana-Raisin Chutney (page 192).

Yield: 6 servings

Soak the lemon grass in ¼ cup (60 ml) of the coconut milk for 30 minutes. Strain, reserving both the lemon grass and the coconut milk.

Bring the water to a boil in a large saucepan. Add the mussels and clams and cook, covered, until the shells open. Remove the meat (discard any shellfish that don't open). Strain the liquid through a fine sieve.

Put the garlic, onion, and nuts in a food processor and process until finely chopped, about 20 seconds, stopping to scrape down the sides of the bowl as necessary. Add the cumin, coriander, curry, red-pepper flakes, salt, and the reserved ¼ cup (60 ml) coconut milk. Process to a smooth paste, about 30 seconds.

Heat the oil in a large sauté pan set over medium heat, add the spice paste and the reserved lemon grass, and stir-fry 2 minutes. Add the remaining 1¼ cups (315 ml) coconut milk and vinegar, and bring to a boil. Cook about 5 minutes, stirring constantly. Add the mussels, clams, shrimp, scallops, and shellfish-cooking liquid. Cook, stirring, until the shrimp and scallops are cooked through, about 5 minutes. Remove the lemon grass before serving.

SPICY COCONUT OPAKAPAKA

6 opakapaka steaks, about 6 ounces/
   170 g each
1 tablespoon macadamia or other nut oil
Salt and pepper
2 tablespoons vegetable oil
1 medium red onion, chopped
2 scallions, thinly sliced
1$^1/_2$ cups (140 g) shredded unsweetened
   coconut
2-inch (5-cm) piece gingerroot, grated
4 cloves garlic, chopped
3 green chilies, seeded and chopped
$^1/_2$ teaspoon chili powder
Grated zest and juice of 1 lime
3 tablespoons water
3 tablespoons chopped cilantro
   (fresh coriander)
3 medium tomatoes, seeded and cut into
   $^1/_4$-inch (6-mm) dice

Opakapaka, or pink snapper, with its sweet, tender, and juicy white flesh, is probably the most popular choice when it appears on the menus of island restaurants. As it is not always available, it is worth trying should you come across it.

Yield: 6 servings

Preheat the oven to 350°F (175°C). Brush the fish with the nut oil, arrange it in an oiled baking dish in one layer, and season with salt and pepper.

Heat the vegetable oil in a medium sauté pan set over medium heat and sauté the onion 5 minutes, or until soft. Add the scallion, coconut, ginger, garlic, chilies, and chili powder. Cook, stirring, 3 minutes, or until golden brown. Stir in the lime zest and juice and water, cover, and simmer 10 minutes, or until the coconut softens. Stir in the cilantro and tomato.

Spoon the mixture over the fish. Bake about 20 minutes, or until the fish begins to flake. (Lightly cover with aluminum foil if the coconut begins to brown too much.) Serve with tossed greens.

opakapaka

ONAGA WITH CILANTRO SAUCE

8 tablespoons (1 stick) (115 g) unsalted
    butter plus more for buttering
    baking dish
4 onaga fillets, about 5 ounces/150 g each
Salt and ground black pepper
1/4 cup (60 ml) water
1/2 cup (20 g) cilantro (fresh coriander)
3/4 cup (180 ml) heavy (double) cream
1 medium daikon or turnip, peeled and
    cut into large oval shapes
2 medium carrots, cut into 1/4-inch
    (6-mm) slices on the diagonal
12 pearl onions, peeled
1 tablespoon freshly squeezed
    lemon juice
Cilantro sprigs and lemon slices
    for garnish

Tender, moist, mild-flavored onaga, or ruby snapper, works best prepared simply, as in this dish. Serve with plain rice.

Yield: 4 servings

Preheat the oven to 300°F (150°C) and lightly butter a shallow baking dish. Arrange the fish in a single layer, sprinkle with salt and pepper, dot with 1 tablespoon of the butter, and pour the water over it. Cover with wax paper and cook 10 minutes, or until opaque. Remove the fish with a slotted spatula, and strain the liquid into a small saucepan.

Put the cilantro in a food processor and process to finely chop. Add 5 tablespoons butter and process until green, about 12 seconds, stopping to scrape down the sides of the bowl as necessary. Add salt and pepper to taste.

Melt the remaining 2 tablespoons of the butter in a medium, heavy sauté pan. Stir in the cream. Add the daikon, carrots, and onions, cover, and cook until tender, about 6 minutes. Remove the vegetables with a slotted spoon and reserve. Add the liquid to the saucepan with the fish-cooking liquid. Cook over medium heat until reduced to 3/4 cup (180 ml), about 5 minutes. Whisk in the lemon juice and cilantro butter. Stir in the reserved vegetables and heat through.

To serve, divide the sauce evenly among 4 warmed plates, arrange the vegetables attractively on one side, and place a fillet on top of the sauce. Garnish with a sprig of cilantro and a lemon slice.

SPICE ISLAND SWORDFISH SKEWERS

1½ pounds (675 g) swordfish steak,
   cut into 1-inch (2.5-cm) cubes
1 cup (230 g) plain yogurt
4 cloves garlic, thinly sliced
1 tablespoon ground coriander
1 teaspoon ground cumin
1 teaspoon ground cardamom
½ teaspoon ground cinnamon
½ teaspoon ground black pepper
½ teaspoon ground clove
1 teaspoon salt
2 jalapeño peppers, seeded and chopped
1 lime, quartered and very thinly sliced

With its aromatic mix of spices, this dish conjures up visions of spice-laden galleons plowing through tropical waters, going from island to island trading Western goods for exotic foods. Serve the kebabs on a bed of rice accompanied by Jícama and Onion Pickle (page 196).

Yield: 4 servings

Thread the fish on skewers and place them in a single layer in a nonreactive baking dish.

Combine the yogurt, garlic, coriander, cumin, cardamom, cinnamon, pepper, clove, and salt, mix well, and pour over the kebabs. Cover with plastic wrap (cling film) and refrigerate 3 hours.

Preheat the broiler (griller). Cook the fish 3 minutes and turn. Sprinkle with the jalapeño, baste with the remaining marinade, and top with the lime. Broil 3 to 4 minutes, or until the fish just begins to flake.

jalapeño peppers

ONO WITH MACADAMIA NUTS AND LIME

1/4 cup (60 ml) olive oil
3 medium onions, thinly sliced
1 cup (115 g) coarsely chopped
    macadamia nuts
1/2 teaspoon ground turmeric
1/2 teaspoon ground cinnamon
1/2 teaspoon ground cumin
1/2 teaspoon ground black pepper
1/2 teaspoon salt
4 ono fillets, 6 ounces/170 g each
2 tablespoons vegetable oil
Juice of 1 lime
Lime slices for garnish

Ono, also called wahoo, has a white, flaky flesh that absorbs the delicious flavors of the spice blend in this recipe very quickly. Serve with a light grain such as couscous, or with quinoa and Baked Eggplant with Sun-Dried Tomato Sauce (page 169).

Yield: 4 servings

Heat the olive oil in a medium sauté pan and sauté the onions until soft, about 10 minutes. Remove from the heat and stir in the nuts, turmeric, cinnamon, cumin, pepper, and salt.

Heat the vegetable oil in a large sauté pan set over medium heat and cook the fish about 4 minutes on each side, or until it flakes. Sprinkle with lime juice on both sides.

To serve, spoon about 1/4 cup (30 g) of the onion mixture into the center of each plate, place the fish on top, then distribute about 2 tablespoons of the mixture attractively over it. Garnish with lime slices.

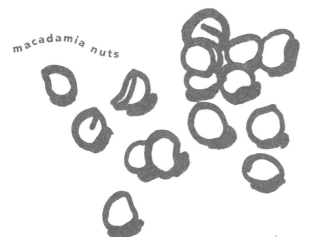

macadamia nuts

lime

MAHIMAHI IN TANGERINE SAUCE

8 dried black mushrooms

8 water chestnuts, sliced

4 scallions, sliced on the diagonal

4 cloves garlic, finely chopped

1-inch (2.5-cm) piece gingerroot,
    finely chopped

1 tablespoon grated tangerine zest

1/4 cup (60 ml) freshly squeezed
    tangerine juice

1 cup (250 ml) fish stock or clam juice

2 tablespoons mirin

2 tablespoons light soy sauce

2 teaspoons Asian sesame oil

1 teaspoon red-pepper flakes

1/2 teaspoon sugar

1/2 cup plus 1 tablespoon (75 g)
    cornstarch (cornflour)

2 tablespoons water

4 mahimahi fillets, 6 ounces/170 g each

1/4 cup (60 ml) vegetable oil

Salt

**Tangerine heightens the natural sweet taste of fresh mahimahi.
Serve with Pan-Fried Noodles (page 183) and steamed vegetables.**

Yield: 4 servings

Soak the mushrooms in hot water 30 minutes. Drain, cut out and discard the stems, and slice the mushrooms into thin strips. Put the mushroom, water chestnut, and scallion in a small bowl and set aside. Put the garlic, ginger, and tangerine zest in another small bowl and set aside. Put the tangerine juice, fish stock, mirin, soy sauce, sesame oil, red-pepper flakes, and sugar in another small bowl, stir well, and set aside. Stir together the 1 tablespoon cornstarch with the water in another small bowl and set aside.

Sift the remaining 1/2 cup (75 g) cornstarch onto a plate. Dip the fish in the cornstarch to coat, shaking off the excess.

Heat the vegetable oil in a large, heavy skillet set over high heat until it is very hot and sauté the fish about 2 minutes on each side, or until cooked through. Place on paper towels (kitchen paper) to drain.

Reduce the heat to medium. Cook the garlic mixture a few seconds, stirring. Add the mushroom mixture and cook, stirring 10 seconds more. Add the fish stock mixture and bring to a boil. Stir in the cornstarch slurry, a teaspoon at a time, to thicken the sauce slightly. Add salt to taste.

Return the fish to the pan to heat through, turning once. Transfer the fish to warmed serving plates and top with the remaining sauce.

SESAME-GINGER-CRUSTED AHI

1/2 onion, coarsely chopped

4 cloves garlic, finely chopped

2 tablespoons chopped cilantro (fresh coriander)

1 tablespoon freshly squeezed lime juice

1 mango, coarsely chopped

1/4 pineapple, cut into 1-inch (2.5-cm) cubes

1 1/2-inch (4-cm) piece gingerroot, peeled and sliced

2 tablespoons raw sesame seeds

1/2 teaspoon salt

1/4 teaspoon ground black pepper

8 tablespoons (1 stick) (115 g) unsalted butter, at room temperature

2 1/2-inch- (6.5-cm-) thick ahi steaks, about 8 ounces (230 g) each

3 tablespoons olive oil

4 ounces (115 g) mesclun

12 endive leaves

Lime wedges for garnish

Use only the finest quality ahi for this dish. You can prepare the salsa and crust mixture well in advance, and sear, slice, and arrange the fish just before serving.

Yield: 4 servings

Put the onion, half the garlic, the cilantro, lime juice, mango, and pineapple in a food processor and pulse 8 times. Refrigerate the salsa until ready to use.

Put the ginger, the remaining garlic, the sesame seeds, salt, and pepper in the food processor and process 5 seconds. Transfer to a medium bowl. Add the butter and stir to blend.

Lay a sheet of wax paper approximately 12 inches (30.5 cm) long on a work surface. Place one ahi steak on the lower half of the sheet and spread a quarter of the butter mixture over it.

Fold the top half of the sheet over it and pat gently to form an even layer. Turn the package upside down, pull back the paper, and spread another quarter of the mixture over the other side of the fish. Carefully spread some around the edges, so that the whole steak is enclosed. Fold the paper back over the fish, patting the top, bottom, and sides, and place it in the freezer until the butter mixture is firm to the touch, approximately 20 minutes. Repeat with the remaining steak.

Heat the olive oil in a large nonstick pan and sear the fish about 2 minutes on each side. Transfer to a cutting board and slice 1/8-inch (3-mm) thick. The center should still be raw.

Divide the mesclun among 4 plates. Arrange the endive attractively and spoon a little salsa onto each leaf. Place slices of ahi across the salad and garnish with lime wedges.

GRILLED FISH IN HOT TAMARIND SAUCE

1 tablespoon tamarind paste

¹/₄ cup (60 ml) hot water

Juice of 1 lime

5 tablespoons vegetable oil plus more
     for basting

4 steaks firm-fleshed fish, such as ahi,
     ono, or swordfish, about 5 ounces/
     140 g each

¹/₂ medium onion, thinly sliced

4 scallions, sliced

1-inch (2.5-cm) piece gingerroot, grated

2 cloves garlic, thinly sliced

Grated zest of ¹/₂ lime

1 teaspoon mustard seeds

¹/₂ teaspoon cayenne

1 tablespoon tomato paste

2 medium tomatoes, seeded and cut into
     ¹/₄-inch (6-mm) dice

**The flavors in this dish are quite exotic, but it is surprisingly easy
and quick to prepare.**

Yield: 4 servings

Soak the tamarind paste in the hot water for 30 minutes. Strain the
mixture, pressing the juice from the pulp. Discard the pulp and set
aside the liquid.

Remove 2 tablespoons of the lime juice and reserve. Combine
the remaining lime juice with 2 tablespoons of the oil and brush the
mixture on the fish.

Heat 2 tablespoons oil in a small sauté pan set over medium-
high heat and cook the onion and scallion 3 minutes, or until softened. Add the ginger, garlic, lime zest, and mustard seeds, and cook
2 minutes more. Add the tamarind liquid, cayenne, and tomato
paste, stir well, and bring to a boil. Reduce the heat, add the tomato,
and simmer about 5 minutes, until the sauce thickens slightly.

Heat the grill and brush the fish with the remaining 1 tablespoon oil. Grill about 5 minutes on each side, taking care not to
overcook, basting occasionally with more oil.

Transfer to plates and distribute the sauce evenly over each steak.

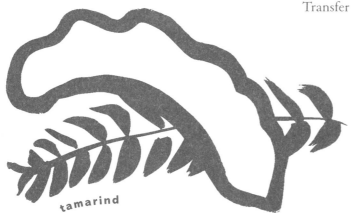

tamarind

GRILLED SALMON WITH CITRUS AIOLI

3 cloves garlic, peeled
1/2 teaspoon salt
1/2 teaspoon ground black pepper
2 large egg yolks, at room temperature
3/4 cup (180 ml) plus 1 tablespoon
   olive oil
Zest of 1/2 orange
Zest of 1/4 lime
1/4 cup (60 ml) freshly squeezed
   orange juice
1 tablespoon freshly squeezed lime juice
4 salmon fillets, about 5 ounces/
   140 g each
Salt and ground black pepper

Lively citrus flavors complement the salmon in this quick-to-prepare dish. Serve with Rosemary Scallop Potato Pie (page 163).

Yield: 4 servings

Put the garlic in a blender with the salt and pepper, and pulse to chop. Add the egg yolks and with the blender running on medium pour the 3/4 cup (180 ml) oil in a thin stream slowly onto the eggs. When blended and thickened, add the orange and lime zests and juices, and blend until incorporated. Refrigerate until ready to use.

Heat the grill, brush the salmon on both sides with the 1 tablespoon oil, and season lightly with salt and pepper.

Grill about 6 minutes on each side, being careful not to overcook. Serve with the citrus aioli.

SPICY SHRIMP SAUTÉ

2 tablespoons olive oil

4 cloves garlic, finely chopped

1 medium onion, finely chopped

1 teaspoon ground cumin

1 teaspoon ground coriander

1/2 teaspoon red-pepper flakes

1/2 cup (20 g) loosely packed flat-leaf
    parsley, finely chopped

2 pounds (900 g) medium shrimp
    (prawns), shells on

1 teaspoon salt

1/2 teaspoon ground black pepper

3 tablespoons freshly squeezed lime juice

Serve these shrimp with Banana, Lentil, and Rosemary Salad (page 85) and crusty bread for a light, spicy lunch.

Yield: 6 servings

Heat the oil in a large sauté pan set over medium heat and sauté the garlic and onion 1 minute. Add the cumin, coriander, and red-pepper flakes and sauté 1 minute more. Add the parsley, shrimp, salt, pepper, and lime juice and sauté 2 minutes. Cover, reduce the heat to low, and continue cooking until the shrimp are heated through, about 4 minutes.

shrimp

SEARED MARINATED SWORDFISH

1/2 cup (120 ml) olive oil

1/2 cup (120 ml) Asian sesame oil

4 thin slices lime

2 tablespoons chopped cilantro
(fresh coriander)

1 teaspoon green peppercorns packed in
brine, drained and crushed

1 teaspoon thyme

1 teaspoon coriander seeds

4 swordfish steaks, about 6 ounces/
170 g each

1/4 cup (60 ml) mirin

1/4 cup (60 ml) soy sauce

2 teaspoons Dijon mustard

Ground black pepper

6 tablespoons (90 ml) vegetable oil

Lime wedges and cilantro sprigs
for garnish

Serve this with a vegetable stir-fry of bok choy and lotus root, and steamed rice.

Yield: 4 servings

Combine the olive oil, 2 tablespoons of the sesame oil, the lime slices, chopped cilantro, green peppercorns, thyme, and coriander in a small bowl. Put the fish in a sealable plastic freezer bag and pour in the marinade. Seal and cover with another plastic bag. Refrigerate and allow to marinate 3 hours.

Put the mirin, soy sauce, mustard, and black pepper in a food processor, and process to blend. With the motor running, add the vegetable oil and remaining 6 tablespoons (90 ml) sesame oil in a steady stream, processing until emulsified, about 5 seconds. Transfer to a sauce bowl.

Preheat a grill or a large cast-iron sauté pan.

Drain the fish and pat dry with paper towels (kitchen paper). Sear until the outside is crusted over and the center is just cooked, about 2 minutes on each side. Do not overcook. Garnish with the lime wedges and cilantro sprigs, and serve with the sauce.

POULTRY

Many
of the rec-
ipes in this
s e c t i o n
have a long
list of ingredi-
ents, but when
you examine them, you
will find that most of the items are spices. You probably have most of them on your spice rack already, such as cumin, red-pepper flakes, paprika,
cinnamon, curry powder, and cayenne. Cardamom, a
highly fragrant scented seed pod available either in pods
or ground to a fine powder, may not be as familiar.
In India they chew on the pods after eating to
freshen the breath, just as Chinese court-
iers used to keep whole cloves in
their mouths when speaking to
the emperor. Ground coriander is another less
f a m i l i a r
spice. It
comes from
the crushed seeds

of the cilantro plant and imparts a sweet, lemony-sage flavor quite different from the leaves.

Spice blends are responsible for some of the world's great tastes, such as curry, an Indian mix of such spices as cumin, coriander, cinnamon, clove, turmeric, mustard, ginger, and chilies. Different regions or countries with Indian-influenced cuisines will emphasize some spice flavors more than others. For example, northern Indian curries will often include caraway and nutmeg, while southern curries will soothe and mellow out the heat with the addition of coconut milk, as in Duck in Coconut Sauce (page 140). Indonesian curries, on the other hand, emphasize cardamom and fresh ginger among their flavors, as in Spicy Coconut-Cashew Chicken (page 142), Tropical Spicy Chicken (page 144), and Chicken in Sun-Dried-Tomato Sauce (page 145).

Another spice blend that appears frequently in the cooking of Asia and the Pacific is Chinese five-spice powder. This blend of hot Szechwan pepper, cinnamon, clove, star anise, and ginger cannot help transforming the simplest dish into something provocative and interesting, as in Sesame Chicken Wings (page 148) and Roast Duck in Tangerine Sauce (page 146).

PAPAYA CHICKEN SKEWERS

2 pounds (900 g) boneless, skinless
    chicken breast, cut into ³/₄-inch
    (2-cm) cubes
1¹/₂ cups (340 g) plain yogurt
2 cups (450 g) mashed ripe papaya
    (pawpaw)
2-inch (5-cm) piece gingerroot, grated
3 cloves garlic, finely chopped
1 teaspoon cayenne
1 tablespoon ground coriander
¹/₄ cup (60 ml) freshly squeezed lime
    juice
3 tablespoons vegetable oil
Salt
Lime wedges for garnish

These tasty skewers can be prepared ahead, making them ideal for a party or barbecue. Serve over plain rice with Tomato-Ginger Salsa (page 191).

Yield: 6 servings

Thread the chicken cubes onto short skewers and place them in a shallow glass baking dish. In a medium bowl combine the yogurt, papaya, ginger, garlic, cayenne, coriander, lime juice, and oil, and season with salt. Pour the mixture over the chicken, turning the skewers to coat completely. Cover with plastic wrap (cling film) and refrigerate at least 8 hours.

Grill the chicken until cooked through, about 6 minutes, turning often and basting occasionally with the remaining marinade. Garnish with lime wedges.

papaya

DUCK IN COCONUT SAUCE

2 tablespoons vegetable oil
4¹/2-pound (2-kg) duck, quartered
    and skinned
1 cup (250 ml) water
1 teaspoon mustard seeds
1 medium onion, finely chopped
4 cloves garlic, peeled and crushed
2-inch (5-cm) piece gingerroot, grated
1 teaspoon red-pepper flakes
2 teaspoons ground cumin
1 tablespoon ground coriander
1 teaspoon ground turmeric
2 tablespoons rice vinegar
2 cups (500 ml) coconut milk
Salt
Paprika
2 tablespoons shredded coconut, toasted
Lime wedges for garnish

This tropical-flavored dish is quick to prepare and a good alternative to the usual roast duck. Serve with a crunchy green papaya salad and a light grain such as quinoa or couscous.

Yield: 4 servings

Preheat the oven to 350°F (175°C). Heat the oil in a large sauté pan set over high heat and brown the duck on both sides, about 5 minutes. Transfer the duck to a covered casserole (do not wash the sauté pan), add the water, cover, and bake 30 minutes, or until tender. Remove from the oven and keep warm.

While the duck is cooking, fry the mustard seeds in the oil in the sauté pan 1 minute, or until they begin to pop. Add the onion and cook, stirring, over medium heat until soft, about 5 minutes. Add the garlic, ginger, red-pepper flakes, cumin, coriander, and turmeric, and cook 2 minutes. Stir in the vinegar.

Transfer the mixture to a food processor (do not wash the pan). Pulse, then process until the mixture is a paste. With the motor running, pour in the coconut milk and process until blended, stopping to scrape down the sides of the bowl as necessary. Add salt to taste. Transfer back to the sauté pan and bring to a boil. Add the duck pieces, cover, reduce the heat, and simmer about 30 minutes, or until the duck is very tender and the sauce has thickened. To serve, sprinkle with paprika and garnish with the shredded coconut and lime wedges.

SPICY LEMON-GINGER CHICKEN STIR-FRY

Yield: 6 servings

2 tablespoons vegetable oil
6 scallions, thinly sliced
6 boneless, skinless chicken breasts, sliced
   1/4-inch (6-mm) thick
4 cloves garlic, thinly sliced
3-inch (7.5-cm) piece gingerroot, grated
2 teaspoons ground cumin
3 tablespoons Spicy Nut Paste (page 143)
1/4 cup (60 ml) freshly squeezed
   lemon juice
1/2 cup (120 ml) water
Salt

Heat the oil in a large, heavy sauté pan set over medium heat and cook the scallion until soft, about 3 minutes. Remove it with a slotted spoon and set aside. Add the chicken, raise the heat to high, and stir-fry until cooked through, about 5 minutes. Add the garlic, ginger, cumin, and Spicy Nut Paste and cook 1 minute. Add the lemon juice and water, season with salt, cover, reduce the heat to low, and cook 10 minutes. Add the reserved scallion and serve with rice.

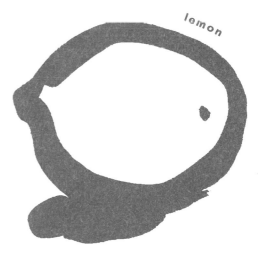

lemon

SPICY COCONUT-CASHEW CHICKEN

2 tablespoons vegetable oil

*6 chicken thighs and drumsticks,
    skin removed*

1 onion, finely chopped

3 cloves garlic, finely chopped

*1 tablespoon finely chopped jalapeño
    pepper*

*1 medium tomato, peeled, seeded, and
    cut into ¼-inch (6-mm) dice*

½ cup (85 g) roasted cashews

1 cup (250 ml) coconut milk

*½ cup (115 g) Spicy Nut Paste
    (recipe follows)*

Salt

This fragrant dish is best served with plain rice and a simple cucumber-mint salad to contrast with the rich sauce.

Yield: 6 servings

Heat the oil in a large, heavy sauté pan set over medium heat and brown the chicken all over. Remove the chicken and cook the onion and garlic 2 minutes, or until soft. Add the jalapeño, tomato, cashews, coconut milk, and Spicy Nut Paste, and season with salt. Add the chicken, cover, reduce the heat to low, and cook 10 minutes, or until the chicken is heated through.

coconut

SPICY NUT PASTE

2 tablespoons vegetable oil
1 teaspoon ground cumin
1 teaspoon cardamom seeds
1 teaspoon powdered mustard
1 teaspoon ground black pepper
2 large cloves garlic, chopped
1-inch (2.5-cm) piece gingerroot,
    chopped
$^1/_2$ cup (85 g) raw cashews
$^1/_4$ cup (60 ml) hot water

Yield: 1 cup (230 g)

Heat the oil in a small, heavy sauté pan set over medium-low heat and cook the cumin, cardamom, mustard, and pepper 5 minutes, shaking the pan and taking care not to allow the spices to burn. Add the garlic and ginger, cook 2 minutes more. Transfer the mixture to a food processor, pulse, then process until finely and evenly chopped, stopping to scrape down the sides of the bowl as necessary. Add the cashews and process 30 seconds. Add the hot water and grind to a smooth paste. Will keep up to one month refrigerated in an airtight container.

TROPICAL SPICY CHICKEN

3-pound (1.4-kg) chicken, cut into
    8 pieces, skin removed
2 tablespoons freshly squeezed lime juice
Salt
1 medium onion, peeled and cut
    into quarters
2-inch (5-cm) piece gingerroot, grated
1 teaspoon paprika
$1/2$ teaspoon ground cumin
$1/2$ teaspoon ground cardamom
$1/2$ teaspoon ground cinnamon
$1/2$ teaspoon ground coriander
$1/4$ teaspoon ground clove
$1/2$ teaspoon ground black pepper
2 cups (450 g) fruit yogurt, such as
    strawberry, mango, peach, or papaya
1 tablespoon chopped cilantro
    (fresh coriander)
Lime wedges for garnish

Exotic and exciting, this dish is best served with Papaya-Mango-Mint (page 188) or Mango-Pineapple Salsa (page 188).

Yield: 4 servings

Slash the meaty parts of the chicken pieces 2 or 3 times on each side and place the chicken in a shallow glass baking dish. Sprinkle with lime juice and season with salt. Put the onion, ginger, paprika, cumin, cardamom, cinnamon, coriander, clove, pepper, and yogurt in a food processor, pulse, then process until smooth. Pour the mixture over the chicken, turning the pieces to coat all sides. Cover with plastic wrap (cling film) and refrigerate at least 8 hours.

Preheat the oven to 400°F (200°C). Drain the chicken and cook 30 minutes, or until tender. Sprinkle with the cilantro and garnish with lime wedges.

CHICKEN IN SUN-DRIED-TOMATO SAUCE

5 sun-dried tomatoes

8-ounce (230-g) can plum (egg)
　tomatoes, drained

2-inch (5-cm) piece gingerroot, grated

3 cloves garlic, peeled

2 tablespoons soy sauce

Juice of 1 lime

Juice of 1 lemon

1 teaspoon cayenne

$^1/_2$ teaspoon ground cardamom

$^1/_2$ teaspoon ground cinnamon

$^1/_4$ teaspoon ground clove

$^1/_2$ teaspoon ground cumin

$^1/_2$ teaspoon ground coriander

2 teaspoons sugar

8 small skinless, boneless chicken breasts

This East-meets-West chicken dish is a refreshing change for people who love red sauce but want to try something somewhat different. Serve with rice or noodles and Bamboo Shoot Pickle (page 195).

Yield: 4 servings

Soak the sun-dried tomatoes in hot water 10 minutes. Drain and transfer to a food processor along with the plum tomatoes, ginger, and garlic, and process until finely chopped. Add the soy sauce, lime juice, lemon juice, cayenne, cardamom, cinnamon, clove, cumin, coriander, and sugar, and process 10 seconds, or until well blended. Arrange the chicken breasts in one layer in a shallow glass baking dish and pour the mixture over it. Cover with plastic wrap (cling film) and refrigerate 2 hours, turning the chicken once.

　　Preheat the oven to 400°F (200°C). Cook the chicken 30 minutes, or until chicken cooks through, basting with the sauce 2 or 3 times.

ROAST DUCK IN TANGERINE SAUCE

THE DUCK

4¹/2-pound (2-kg) duck

4¹/₂-pound (2-kg) duck

1 tablespoon Chinese five-spice powder

2 teaspoons ground cinnamon

1 teaspoon ground cardamom

1 teaspoon ground cumin

1 teaspoon ground coriander

1 teaspoon ground black pepper

THE STUFFING

¹/₂ cup (55 g) couscous

1¹/₂ cups (375 ml) hot water

1 medium onion, finely chopped

¹/₃ cup (45 g) chopped macadamia nuts

¹/₃ cup (55 g) chopped roasted cashews

¹/₃ cup (45 g) chopped blanched almonds

3 tablespoons chopped cilantro
  (fresh coriander)

¹/₂ teaspoon paprika

¹/₂ teaspoon salt

1 large egg yolk

(continued on next page)

Surprisingly easy to prepare, with a delightful combination of flavors and textures, this is a perfect dish for a special occasion. With its light and intriguing couscous-nut stuffing and zesty tangerine-lime sauce, this dish gives a fresh new twist to the old standard *canard à l'orange*. Chickpea flour is available at health food stores.

Yield: 4 servings

Preheat the oven to 400°F (200°C). Prick the duck skin all over with a fork. Combine the five-spice powder, cinnamon, cardamom, cumin, coriander, and pepper, and rub the mixture onto the skin. Set aside in the refrigerator.

Soak the couscous in the hot water 30 minutes. Add the onion, macadamia nuts, cashews, almonds, cilantro, paprika, salt, and egg yolk, and blend well.

Stuff the duck with the couscous mixture, truss, and place in a roasting pan. Roast 1¹/₄ hours, or until tender, removing the fat from the pan as it accumulates. Remove the duck from the oven and keep warm until ready to serve.

While the duck is cooking, make the sauce. Heat the oil in a medium sauté pan set over medium-high heat and cook the onion until soft, about 5 minutes. Stir in the garlic, ginger, turmeric, coriander, and chick-pea flour. Transfer the mixture to a food processor, pulse, then process to a paste, stopping to scrape down the sides of the bowl as necessary. With the motor running, pour in the cream and process until well blended. Return the sauce to the pan and heat gently without boiling. Season with salt and simmer 3 minutes. Add the tangerine and lime juice, stirring constantly, and remove from the heat.

Carve the duck and arrange on plates with stuffing. Reheat the sauce in the microwave or a double boiler, being careful not to allow it to boil. Pour sauce over the duck and sprinkle with the cilantro.

(continued from previous page)

THE SAUCE

2 tablespoons vegetable oil

1 medium onion, chopped

2 cloves garlic, crushed

1-inch (2.5-cm) piece gingerroot, grated

1 teaspoon ground turmeric

2 teaspoons ground coriander

1 tablespoon chickpea flour or masa
   harina (tortilla cornflour)

1½ cups (375 ml) heavy cream

Salt

½ cup (120 ml) freshly squeezed
   tangerine juice

2 tablespoons freshly squeezed lime juice

1 tablespoon chopped cilantro
   (fresh coriander)

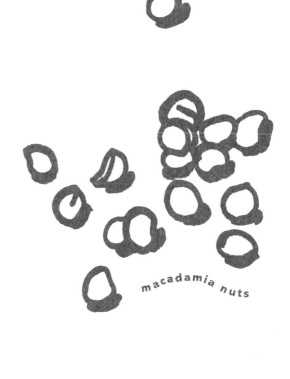

macadamia nuts

tangerine

SESAME CHICKEN WINGS

1 teaspoon salt
2 tablespoons light soy sauce
2 tablespoons honey
2 tablespoons mirin
$1/2$ teaspoon grated gingerroot
$1/2$ teaspoon Chinese five-spice powder
2 tablespoons vegetable oil
12 chicken wings, split
2 tablespoon sesame seeds

Sticky fun to eat with your fingers, these wings are especially loved by children.

Yield: 3 servings

In a shallow glass baking dish, stir together the salt, soy sauce, honey, mirin, ginger, five-spice powder, and oil. Add the chicken and toss to coat.

Cover with plastic wrap (cling film) and refrigerate 3 to 8 hours, turning occasionally.

Preheat the oven to 400°F (200°C). Sprinkle the chicken with sesame seeds on both sides. Bake 30 minutes, or until done, brushing occasionally with the marinade.

CHICKEN SATAY

PEANUT SATAY SAUCE

2 tablespoons tamarind paste

1/4 cup (60 ml) hot water

2 tablespoons vegetable oil

1 medium onion, finely chopped

4 cloves garlic, finely chopped

1 teaspoon grated gingerroot

1 teaspoon red-pepper flakes

2 tablespoons freshly squeezed lime juice

Grated zest of 1/2 lime

2 tablespoons chopped lemon grass

2 teaspoons curry powder

1 cup (250 ml) coconut milk

3 tablespoons firmly packed brown sugar

1 cup (230 g) chunky peanut butter

6 skinless, boneless chicken breasts,
    cut into 3/4-inch (2-cm) cubes

1 tablespoon vegetable oil

2-inch (5-cm) piece cinnamon stick

An island favorite, satay sauce accompanies a variety of Thai dishes and works equally well with chicken, beef, and tofu. The addition of tamarind and lemon grass here adds a vibrant, fresh, tangy flavor. I like to serve satay accompanied by a fresh salsa, such as Asian Salsa (page 189) or Papaya-Pineapple Salsa (page 192).

Yield: 6 servings

Put the tamarind paste to soak in the hot water.

Heat 2 tablespoons of the oil in a medium saucepan set over medium heat and cook the onion 5 minutes, or until soft. Add garlic, ginger, red-pepper flakes, lime juice, zest, lemon grass, and curry, and cook 1 minute. Add the coconut milk and cook 5 minutes. Add the tamarind with its liquid, the sugar, and peanut butter, and bring to a boil. Transfer to a food processor and process until smooth.

Thread the chicken onto small skewers. Heat 1 tablespoon oil in a large sauté pan set over medium heat. Working in batches, place as many skewers as will fit without crowding in the pan and cook 5 minutes, turning frequently so they do not burn. Return all the skewers to the pan, add the sauce and the cinnamon, and bring to a boil. Reduce the heat and simmer 15 minutes. Remove the cinnamon stick and serve.

LIME-CILANTRO CHICKEN

3 tablespoons vegetable oil
6 chicken thighs and drumsticks,
    skin removed
1 tablespoon finely chopped gingerroot
6 cloves garlic, finely chopped
1 jalapeño pepper, seeded and finely
    chopped
1 tablespoon chopped turmeric root or
    ground turmeric
1 1/2 teaspoons ground cumin
1 1/2 teaspoons ground coriander
1 teaspoon red-pepper flakes
Salt and ground black pepper
3/4 cup (180 ml) water
Juice and grated zest of 1 lime
1 cup (40 g) loosely packed cilantro
    (fresh coriander)

Easy to prepare, this is a great dish to serve at a large party, as it can be made a day ahead and is delicious cold, or may be heated right before serving.

Yield: 6 servings

Heat the oil in a large, heavy pan set over medium-high heat and brown the chicken all over. Remove the chicken from the pan and add the ginger, garlic, jalapeño, turmeric, cumin, coriander, and red-pepper flakes, and season with salt and pepper. Cook, stirring, 1 minute. Return the chicken to the pan, pour in the water and lime juice, and bring to a boil. Reduce the heat to medium, add the lime zest, cover, and cook 30 minutes, or until the chicken is cooked through and tender. Stir in cilantro and serve.

cilantro

CURRIED LEMON-LIME CHICKEN

This piquant curry dish is redolent of the exotic aromas of the islands. Serve with fried rice and Tropical-Fruit Salsa (page 190).

Yield: 4 servings

1 medium onion, peeled and quartered

3 cloves garlic, peeled

2-inch (5-cm) piece gingerroot, peeled

1 teaspoon turmeric

1 teaspoon red-pepper flakes

1 teaspoon salt

1 teaspoon sugar

2 cups (500 ml) coconut milk

1 tablespoon vegetable oil

2 teaspoons curry powder

3-pound (1.4 kg) chicken cut into
    16 pieces, skin removed

2 1½-inch (4-cm) strips lemon zest

2 1½-inch (4-cm) strips lime zest

1 tablespoon lemon juice

1 tablespoon lime juice

With the motor running, drop half the onion, 2 of the garlic cloves, the ginger, turmeric, red-pepper flakes, salt, and sugar into a food processor and process 10 seconds, or until finely minced, stopping to scrape down the sides of the bowl as necessary. Add the coconut milk and process 10 seconds more, or until well blended.

Thinly slice the remaining half of the onion and garlic clove. Heat the oil in a large, heavy sauté pan set over medium heat and cook the onions and garlic 1 minute. Add the curry powder and stir until well incorporated. Add the chicken pieces and cook 5 minutes on each side. Add the coconut-milk mixture and turn the chicken pieces to coat. Stir in the lemon and lime zests and juices. Bring to a boil, then reduce the heat, cover, and simmer 10 minutes, basting often with the sauce and turning the chicken after 5 minutes. Remove the cover and cook 15 minutes more, or until the chicken is done.

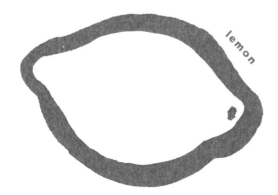

lemon

PIQUANT CHICKEN DRUMSTICKS

12 chicken drumsticks, skinned
8 ounces (230 g) cream cheese
1 medium onion, chopped
1 jalapeño pepper, seeded and chopped
½-inch (1.3-cm) piece gingerroot, grated
2 tablespoons chopped chive
2 tablespoons freshly squeezed lime juice
¼ teaspoon chili powder
¼ teaspoon paprika
2 tablespoons chopped cilantro
   (fresh coriander)
Salt and pepper to taste

Perfect for a barbecue, these drumsticks make a refreshing change from the usual tomato-based barbecue sauces. Serve with Coconut-Mango Salsa (page 191) or Tropical-Fruit Salsa (page 190).

Yield: 6 servings

Slash the meaty parts of the drumsticks 2 or 3 times on both sides and place them in a single layer in a shallow glass baking dish. Put the cream cheese, onion, jalapeño, ginger, chive, lime juice, chili powder, paprika, cilantro, and salt and pepper in a food processor, pulse, then process until smooth, stopping to scrape down the sides of the bowl as necessary. Pour the mixture over the drumsticks, turning to coat. Cover with plastic wrap (cling film) and refrigerate overnight or up to 2 days.

Heat a broiler (griller) or grill and cook the drumsticks 10 to 15 minutes, or until done, basting occasionally with the remaining marinade and turning frequently.

FIERY CHILI CHICKEN WINGS

Juice of 2 limes
2 tablespoons red-pepper flakes
1 tablespoon paprika
Salt to taste
12 chicken wings, split

Quick and easy to prepare, these wings are always a hit. You can adjust the heat to suit your taste by adding more or less red-pepper flakes.

Yield: 4 servings

Combine the lime juice, red-pepper flakes, paprika, and salt in a shallow glass baking dish. Add the chicken wings and turn to coat. Allow to marinate 30 minutes, turning a couple of times. Preheat the broiler (griller) and cook 10 minutes on each side, or until done. Serve at room temperature.

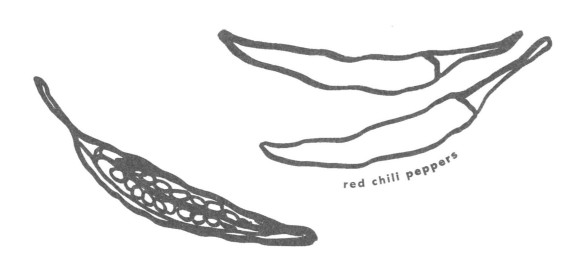

red chili peppers

CURRIED RAGOUT OF CHICKEN WITH BUTTERNUT SQUASH

2 2½-pound (1.1-kg) chickens, cut into
   12 pieces
Salt and coarsely ground black pepper
2 tablespoons vegetable oil
6 tablespoons (90 g) unsalted butter
4 cloves garlic, sliced
3 medium onions, cut into 8 wedges
2 tablespoons curry powder
2 tablespoons tomato paste
¼ teaspoon ground clove
1 teaspoon red-pepper flakes
1 teaspoon ground coriander
1 teaspoon ground cinnamon
2 cups (500 ml) chicken stock
1 butternut (winter) squash (2 pounds/
   900 g), cut into 1-inch (2.5-cm) cubes
2 tablespoons packed dark-brown sugar
1 tablespoon cornstarch (cornflour)
   mixed with 2 tablespoons cold water
½ cup (20 g) coarsely packed chopped
   cilantro (fresh coriander)

A ragout is a hearty stew of meat and vegetables cooked in their own juices. The slow cooking allows the flavors to develop, and it is best served reheated the day after it is made. Serve this with crusty bread to absorb the juices.

Yield: 6 servings

Preheat the oven to 350°F (175°C). Season the chicken with salt and pepper. Heat the oil in a large, heavy sauté pan set over medium-high heat. Working in batches, brown the chicken until golden brown on both sides. Transfer to a large covered casserole.

Discard all the fat from the pan and reduce the heat to medium. Heat 4 tablespoons (55 g) of the butter and cook the garlic and onion until soft but not browned. Stir in the curry powder, tomato paste, clove, red-pepper flakes, coriander, and cinnamon. Add the stock and stir well to combine. When heated through, pour over the chicken in the casserole. Cover and bake 1 hour.

While the chicken is cooking, steam the squash 3 minutes, or until just tender.

Heat the remaining 2 tablespoons butter in a medium sauté pan set over high heat and stir in the sugar. When it is dissolved, add the drained squash. Cook, stirring, until caramelized, about 5 minutes.

Remove the chicken and onion from the casserole with a slotted spoon. Whisk the cornstarch slurry into the liquid, working fast to prevent lumps. Return the chicken and onion to the casserole, add the squash, stir to combine, cover, and bake about 15 minutes to heat through.

When ready to serve, adjust the seasoning and sprinkle with the cilantro.

GRILLED GINGER CHICKEN

3-inch (7.5-cm) piece gingerroot,
    chopped
3 cloves garlic
1/4 cup (60 ml) freshly squeezed
    lime juice
2 tablespoons vegetable oil
1 tablespoon thyme
1 teaspoon salt
1 teaspoon ground black pepper
3-pound (1.4-kg) chicken, cut into
    8 pieces, skin removed

This dish is perfect for a casual barbecue, as the grilled chicken is easy to eat with your fingers. Serve with Pineapple Chutney (page 193), rice, and a tossed green salad.

Yield: 4 servings

Put the ginger and garlic in a food processor and process until finely chopped, stopping to scrape down the sides of the bowl as necessary. Add the lime juice, oil, thyme, salt, and pepper, and process to blend. Place the chicken in a single layer in a shallow glass baking dish. Pour the mixture over the chicken, cover with plastic wrap (cling film), and refrigerate 3 hours, turning the chicken occasionally. Heat the grill and cook until done, turning frequently, about 20 to 30 minutes.

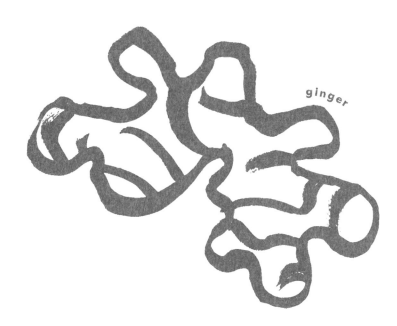

ginger

VEGETABLE ENTRÉES

Devoted exclusively to vegetarian dishes, this chapter offers a sampling of the varied delicious cuisines of the Pacific.

This chapter provides a taste of Mexico and Central America with the exceptional Stuffed Poblano Peppers with Mole (page 160). The velvety, aromatic mole sauce, which includes a small amount of unsweetened chocolate, is traditionally served on festive occasions. Although the list of ingredients may sound daunting, it is well worth a try. Another Mexican treat is Posole (page 159), more familiarly known as hominy. Posole, an ancient Aztec method of preparing corn by soaking it in lime until the kernels swell up, was one of the basic methods the Indians used to prepare and eat corn. Cooked in a rich stock, posole is served surrounded with bowls of salsa, avocado, grated cheese, olives, and diced peppers.

Crossing the Pacific, we encounter the extraordinary cuisine of Southeast Asia. The area is a gold mine of vegetarian dishes, such as my favorite, Evil Jungle

Prince (page 162), a wonderful dish from Thailand, rich and fragrant with fresh herbs, including opal basil, lemon grass, cilantro, and mint. The flavors emanate from a smooth coconut broth filled with lightly cooked, still crunchy vegetables. Served over rice or noodles, this dish is unbeatable for its harmony of blended tastes.

Further north we encounter the Chinese influence on the cuisines of Asia from Hong Kong, Vietnam, Malaysia, Burma, and Indonesia. The uncomplicated Bok Choy Stir-Fry, with lotus root and long beans (page 164), perfectly accompanies Tofu Cakes (page 165) and Papaya-Pineapple Salsa (page 192).

From Indonesia we get the distinct influence of Indian and Arabic cooking, with flavors of tamarind, ginger, cinnamon, and cumin. Eggplant in Cinnamon-Chili Sauce (page 166) conjures up the days when Indonesia was an integral crossroads on the spice route.

POSOLE

2 tablespoons vegetable oil

8 cloves garlic, finely chopped

3 medium onions, cut into ¼-inch
   (6-mm) dice

1 tablespoon chili powder

2 tablespoons ground cumin

4 cups (1 l) vegetable stock

6 tablespoons (60 g) masa harina
   (corn tortilla flour)

1 tablespoon firmly packed brown sugar

1 tablespoon cold water

2 small red chilies

8-ounce (230-g) can yellow hominy,
   drained

8-ounce (230-g) can white hominy,
   drained

8-ounce (230-g) can pinto beans, drained

1 tablespoon salt

1 tablespoon ground black pepper

Posole (poh-zoh-lay) is based upon the specially prepared corn kernel that the Aztecs called nixtamal and we call hominy. The Aztec method of soaking the dried corn kernels in slaked lime resulted in removing the skin and softening the kernel. Serve this posole surrounded by dishes of salsa, guacamole, grated cheese, chopped peppers, sour cream, sliced olives, sliced jalapeños, and hot sauce, and let everyone top their dish with the condiments of their choice.

Yield: 8 to 10 servings

Heat the oil in a large, heavy saucepan set over medium-high heat and sauté the garlic and onion about 3 minutes, or until soft. Stir in the chili powder and cumin, and cook 2 minutes more. Add the stock, lower the heat, and simmer 5 minutes.

Combine the masa harina, sugar, and water, mixing until smooth. Add to the stock, stirring.

Add the chilies and bring the mixture to a boil. Reduce the heat, cover, and simmer 15 minutes. Add the yellow and white hominy and pinto beans.

Cover and continue to simmer over very low heat 30 minutes. Season with salt and pepper, and remove and discard the chilies. Place 2 cups of the mixture in a food processor and purée. Stir the purée back into the pot, and serve.

STUFFED POBLANO PEPPERS WITH MOLE

1 pound (450 g) ripe plantains
12 large poblano peppers
Mole (recipe follows)
6 ounces (170 g) Monterey Jack,
    cut into 12 sticks
3 eggs, lightly beaten
2 cups (280 g) masa harina (corn
    tortilla flour)
Papaya-Mango-Mint Salsa (page 188)
Guacamole (page 197)

This dish combines many of the best foods Mexico has to offer—grilled poblanos, fresh salsa, velvety mole sauce, plantains, and avocado. These grilled stuffed poblanos are rolled in masa harina (corn tortilla flour) and baked, then served topped with guacamole and tropical salsa.

Yield: 6 servings

Slit the skin of each plantain lengthwise and microwave at medium power 4 minutes, or until just soft. Place on a cake rack to cool. When cool, peel and cut into 1/4-inch (6-mm) dice. (Alternatively, place the plantains on a baking sheet and cook at 400°F [200°C] 30 minutes. If knife easily penetrates the flesh, the plantain is done.)

Char the peppers over an open flame. Transfer to a paper or plastic bag, seal, and let sit 15 minutes, or until cooled. Cut off and discard the stem ends, and peel the peppers under running water. Remove the seeds, taking care not to break the flesh.

Preheat oven to 400°F (200°C). Combine the diced plantain with the mole sauce.

Hold a pepper horizontally and fill the lower half with the mixture. Place a stick of cheese on top, then fill the rest of the pepper with the mixture. Repeat with the remaining peppers. Dip each pepper in egg and roll in masa harina. Place the peppers in a single layer in a baking dish and cook 20 minutes, or until golden. Top with Papaya-Mango-Mint Salsa and Guacamole and serve immediately.

MOLE

1 1/2 cups (375 ml) chicken stock
6 small red chili peppers, split and seeded
1 tablespoon vegetable oil
1 medium onion, coarsely chopped
4 cloves garlic, coarsely chopped
1 large tomato, peeled, seeded, and cut
    into 1/4-inch (6-mm) dice
2/3 cup (100 g) blanched almonds
1 cup (140 g) raisins
2 tablespoons sesame seeds
1/4 teaspoon ground clove
1/4 teaspoon ground cinnamon
1/4 teaspoon ground anise
1/4 teaspoon ground coriander
1/2 teaspoon salt
1/4 teaspoon ground black pepper
2 ounces (55 g) unsweetened chocolate
2 tablespoons unsalted butter

Bring the chicken stock to a boil, add the chili peppers, and allow to steep 30 minutes.

Meanwhile, heat the oil in a medium sauté pan set over medium heat and cook the onion and garlic until softened, about 7 minutes. Remove from the heat and stir in the tomato.

Grind the almonds in a food processor until fine, about 15 seconds. Add the raisins and process 15 seconds more. Add the sesame seeds and process to blend, about 10 seconds. Add the clove, cinnamon, anise, coriander, salt, and pepper, and pulse to blend. Add the onion mixture and pulse to blend.

Melt the chocolate and butter together in a microwave or double boiler. Strain the chicken stock, discarding the chilies, and stir the stock into the chocolate mixture. Transfer to a large saucepan, stir in the processed mixture, and simmer over low heat 10 minutes.

plantain

EVIL JUNGLE PRINCE

2 pounds (900 g) mixed vegetables

2 tablespoons vegetable oil

2 stalks lemon grass, cut into 3-inch
    (7.5-cm) pieces

12 kaffir lime leaves or 1 teaspoon each
    grated lemon and lime zest

2 teaspoons red-pepper flakes

2 cups (500 ml) coconut milk

1 cup (40 g) loosely packed basil

1/2 cup (20 g) loosely packed cilantro
    (fresh coriander)

1/4 cup (10 g) loosely packed mint

Salt

Cilantro sprigs for garnish

The aromatic vegetable-and-coconut-milk dish Evil Jungle Prince is served in most of the islands' many Thai restaurants. Choose from the following selection of vegetables: string beans, zucchini (courgette), eggplant (aubergine), onions, green bell peppers (capsicums), carrots, bamboo shoots, miniature corn, water chestnuts, mushrooms, and cucumber.

Yield: 6 servings

Prepare the vegetables by peeling and cutting into thin strips or thin slices cut on the diagonal. Heat the oil in a large saucepan set over medium-high heat and sauté the lemon grass, lime leaves, and red-pepper flakes 3 minutes.

Stir in the coconut milk and bring to a boil.

Add the vegetables, reduce the heat to medium, and cook 10 minutes, or until the vegetables are just tender. Stir in the basil, cilantro, and mint.

Add salt to taste. Serve on a bed of brown rice, and garnish with cilantro sprigs.

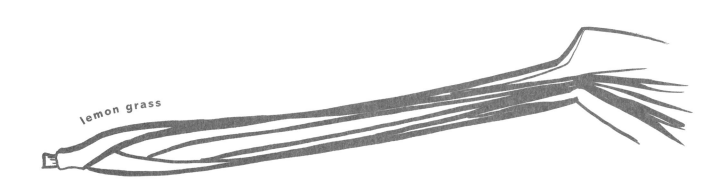

lemon grass

ROSEMARY SCALLOP POTATO PIE

Yield: 4 servings

Butter for greasing baking dish
2 large baking potatoes, peeled
3 tablespoons finely chopped rosemary
1/2 pound (2 sticks) (230 g) unsalted
   butter, melted
Salt and ground black pepper

Preheat the oven to 375°F (190°C) and butter a 9-inch (23-cm) ovenproof glass pie dish.

Using the medium slicing disc of a food processor, slice the potatoes. Stir the rosemary into the melted butter.

Arrange a layer of potatoes on the bottom of the dish, brush with rosemary butter, and sprinkle with salt and pepper. Continue building up layers until all the potatoes are used. Keep back enough rosemary butter to brush the top layer well. Bake 30 minutes, or until crisp and golden brown on top.

BOK CHOY STIR-FRY

1 tablespoon vegetable oil

1 tablespoon Asian sesame oil

3 cloves garlic, thinly sliced

1-inch (2.5-cm) piece gingerroot, peeled and sliced very thin

3 ounces (85 g) long beans or string beans, cut into 1-inch (2.5-cm) lengths

2 small lotus roots, peeled and cut into $^{1}/_{4}$-inch (6-mm) slices

1 small head bok choy, cut into 1-inch (2.5-cm) slices

1 tablespoon vegetarian oyster sauce

2 teaspoons Asian hot chili sauce

1 tablespoon tamari or soy sauce

Versatile bok choy, used throughout Asia, appears similar to chard. The crunchy stalks and leaves have a mild, juicy sweetness and are low in calories and rich in vitamins A and C. Stir-fried with other vegetables, it makes a tasty, light dish.

Yield: 4 servings

Heat the vegetable and sesame oils in a wok or large sauté pan set over medium-high heat and stir-fry the garlic and ginger 1 minute.

Add the beans and lotus root and stir-fry 1 minute.

Add the bok choy and stir-fry 1 minute more. Stir in the oyster sauce, hot sauce, and tamari. Remove from the heat and serve immediately over rice.

sliced lotus root

bok choy

TOFU CAKES

½ cup (120 ml) plus 2 teaspoons
*   vegetable oil*
1 tablespoon fennel seeds
1 cup (55 g) fresh bread crumbs
1 small onion, cut into ¼-inch
*   (6-mm) dice*
½ cup (20 g) loosely packed chopped
*   cilantro (fresh coriander)*
8 ounces (230 g) firm tofu (soybean
*   curd), rinsed, drained, and crumbled*
Salt and pepper to taste
1 large egg, lightly beaten

Tofu, or bean curd, is a staple throughout the Pacific. Try these light, flavorful patties topped with Papaya-Pineapple Salsa (page 192) and served with rice.

Yield: 4 servings

Heat the 2 teaspoons oil in a small, heavy sauté pan set over medium-high heat and sauté the fennel seeds 1 minute. Put the bread crumbs, onion, cilantro, tofu, and salt and pepper in a food processor, pulse 3 times, then process 3 seconds. Transfer the mixture to a bowl and stir in the fennel and egg. Form into 8 patties, place on wax paper, and refrigerate at least 30 minutes.

Heat the ½ cup (120 ml) oil in a small sauté pan set over medium-high heat. (The oil should be about ½ inch [1.3 cm] deep.) Working in batches, fry the patties until golden brown on both sides, about 3 minutes per side, and drain on paper towels (kitchen paper). Serve with salsa and rice.

EGGPLANT IN CINNAMON-CHILI SAUCE

2 tablespoons tamarind paste

$^1/_2$ cup (120 ml) hot water

3 tablespoons vegetable oil

2 medium onions, cut into 8 wedges

2-inch (5-cm) piece gingerroot, grated

2 jalapeño peppers, seeded and finely
   chopped

1 tablespoon cinnamon

2 teaspoons paprika

1 tablespoon ground cumin

1 tablespoon ground coriander

1 teaspoon ground clove

$^3/_4$ cup (180 ml) water

$^1/_4$ cup (60 g) firmly packed dark-
   brown sugar

2 teaspoons salt

1 large eggplant (aubergine), cut into
   1-inch (2.5-cm) cubes

4 ounces (115 g) firm tofu (soybean
   curd), cut into 1-inch (2.5-cm) cubes

**This vibrant dish reflects many of the flavors of the Pacific—
tamarind, ginger, cinnamon, and cumin.**

Yield: 4 servings

Soak the tamarind in the hot water 30 minutes. Strain, pressing on
the pulp to extract the liquid. Discard the pulp, reserving the liquid.

Heat the oil in a large, heavy sauté pan set over medium-high
heat, and sauté the onion and ginger until soft, about 3 minutes.
Add the jalapeño, cinnamon, paprika, cumin, coriander, and clove,
stirring continually. When the onions are well coated with the
spices, add the tamarind-soaking liquid, sugar, and salt. Cook,
stirring, 3 minutes. Add the eggplant, stir to mix well, cover,
reduce the heat, and simmer 30 minutes, or until the eggplant is
tender, stirring occasionally.

Gently fold in the tofu. Raise the heat to medium-high and
cook about 15 minutes, or until the sauce is thick and clings to the
eggplant and tofu. Serve over rice.

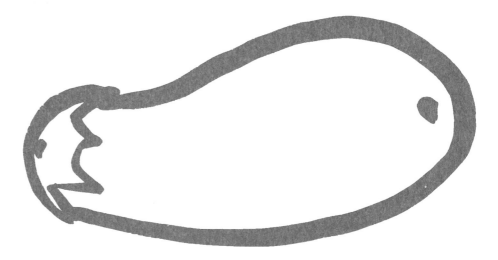

ASIAN RATATOUILLE

1/4 cup (60 ml) olive oil

6 cloves garlic, thinly sliced

3 medium onions, cut into 1/2-inch
    (1.3-cm) dice

1 red bell pepper (capsicum), cut into
    1/2-inch (1.3-cm) squares

1 green bell pepper (capsicum), cut into
    1/2-inch (1.3-cm) squares

2 teaspoons dried rosemary, ground to
    a powder

2 teaspoons salt

2 teaspoons coarsely ground black pepper

3 Japanese eggplants (aubergines), cut
    into 3/4-inch (2-cm) slices

2 medium zucchini (courgettes), cut into
    1/2-inch (1.3-cm) dice

6 plum (egg) tomatoes, seeded and cut
    into 1/2-inch (1.3-cm) dice

1 cup (250 ml) vegetable stock

2 tablespoons mirin

1 cup (40 g) packed cilantro (fresh
    coriander)

1/3 cup (80 ml) Oriental sesame oil

1 teaspoon Oriental hot-chili oil

1/2 recipe Corn Cups or Tartlet Shells
    (recipe follows)

The classic Mediterranean combination of eggplant, zucchini, and tomato is transformed into a Pacific Rim treat with cilantro, sesame, and hot-chili oil. Serve in Tartlet Shells for an entrée (2 shells per serving) or Corn Cups for a pupu.

Yield: 6 servings as an entrée, 12 as a pupu

Heat the olive oil in a large, heavy sauté pan set over medium heat and sauté the garlic 30 seconds. Add the onion, red pepper, green pepper, rosemary, salt, and pepper, stir to coat, and cook 2 minutes. Add the eggplant and cook, stirring, 2 minutes more.

Add the zucchini, tomato, stock, mirin, cilantro, sesame oil, and chili oil, season with salt and pepper, raise the heat to medium-high, and cook, stirring gently and often, 10 minutes more, or until the liquid is syrupy. (The ratatouille can be made up to two days ahead and reheated gently.) Divide the mixture among the warm Corn Cups or Tartlet Shells, and serve immediately.

CORN CUPS OR TARTLET SHELLS

4 tablespoons (¹/2 stick) (55 g) butter,
   at room temperature
6 ounces (170 g) cream cheese, at room
   temperature
2 cups (280 g) all-purpose (plain) flour
   plus more for kneading
1 cup (140 g) fine yellow cornmeal
   (maize flour)
¹/2 teaspoon salt

These pastry shells can be used with just about any savory filling, from ratatouille to chili to chicken salad.

Yield: 24 cups or 12 tartlets

Heat the oven to 400°F (200°C). Put the butter and cream cheese in a food processor and process to combine. Add the flour ¹/2 cup (70 g) at a time, pulsing to combine. Add the cornmeal and salt and pulse until the dough just comes away from the sides of the bowl. Transfer to a floured surface and knead briefly to form a ball.

To make cups, divide the dough into 24 1¹/2-inch (4-cm) balls and place them in small muffin tins. Using your thumb, press the bottom and sides so that the dough comes up to the top of the mold and lines the cup evenly. Bake about 20 minutes, or until golden brown.

To make tartlet shells, divide the dough into 12 balls. Working on a lightly floured surface, roll out one of the balls into a 6-inch (15-cm) circle. Transfer to a 4-inch (10-cm) removable-bottom tart pan, press into place, and trim to leave a ¹/2-inch (1.3-cm) overhang. Fold the overhang inside and press the edges firmly in place. Repeat with the rest of the dough. Prick the bottom and sides with a fork and refrigerate until firm, about 30 minutes.

Place the tart pans on a baking sheet, line with aluminum foil, and fill with dried beans or pie weights. Bake 10 minutes, remove the foil and beans or weights, prick again, and continue baking about 5 minutes more, or until golden brown. Let cool on a rack 5 minutes, then remove from pans. (The shells can be made several hours ahead and rewarmed in a 300°F [150°C] oven a few minutes before filling and serving.)

BAKED EGGPLANT WITH SUN-DRIED-TOMATO SAUCE

4 sun-dried tomatoes

Vegetable oil

4 Japanese eggplants (aubergines),
    cut into ¹/₂-inch (1.3-cm) slices

1 medium onion, thinly sliced

1 green bell pepper (capsicum),
    thinly sliced

¹/₂ teaspoon paprika

1 teaspoon ground cumin

¹/₂ teaspoon ground black pepper

Salt to taste

¹/₂ cup (20 g) loosely packed cilantro
    (fresh coriander), finely chopped

This tasty dish goes well with any grilled or sautéed fish, as well as with chicken or lamb. It can also be coarsely chopped in a food processor and served on toast as an appetizer.

Yield: 2 cups

Soak the sun-dried tomatoes in hot water for 30 minutes. Drain and cut into thin strips.

Preheat the oven to 350°F (175°C) and oil a 9-inch (23-cm) baking dish.

Heat some oil in a large sauté pan set over medium heat. Working in batches, cook the eggplant until soft but not browned, about 3 minutes per side. Transfer the slices to the prepared baking dish as they are cooked. Add more oil to the pan and cook the onions and peppers, stirring, about 3 minutes, or until soft. Stir in the paprika, cumin, pepper, and salt, then spoon the mixture over the eggplant. Add the tomato to the pan and cook about 4 minutes, until just soft but still holding its shape.

Arrange the tomato on top of the eggplant and sprinkle with the cilantro.

Cover tightly with foil and bake 20 minutes, or until the vegetables are tender.

japanese eggplant

PASTA

Although we tend to think Italian when we think of pasta, Asia makes pasta as central to many meals as rice, with a variety of noodles from each country. From Japanese soba, udon, ramen, and somen to the large number of Vietnamese, Thai, and Burmese noodles to Chinese wontons and Filipino lumpia wrappers, pasta plays a large part in the Asian diet. There are noodles that resemble translucent vermicelli made from rice flour, and others that are flat and chewy made from tapioca starch. Some are light and delicate, others substantial and nutty. Throughout Asia there are noodle dishes that are served cold, and others that are served in a bowl of steaming broth with thin slices of vegetables, tofu, meat, or fish, added almost as a garnish, floating on top. Experiment with these dishes and throw a party with a selection of Asian noodles and toppings. You could make a spicy salad (page 90) of cold soba, the thin, brown, nutty buckwheat noodles from Japan, or try udon, which is thick and chewy. Udon can be made ahead and frozen or refrigerated until ready to serve. Prepare Udon with Vegetables and Gado-Gado Sauce (page 177), and serve platters of lightly steamed vegetables in the Indonesian style, with bowls of peanut sauce to top the noodles.

For a deep-green fettuccine topped with a colorful confetti of typical south-of-the-border flavors, try Mexican Fettuccine with Tomatillos and Avocado (page 178). Serve this along with a bowl of tiny shells rich with Pacific flavors, such as Pasta Shells with Citrus-Pepper Shrimp Sauce (page 179), and Soba with Sautéed Vegetables (page 174), flavored with miso (fermented soybean paste) and umeboshi (fruity Japanese fermented plum vinegar). For more ideas, visit your local Asian markets, or look in the Asian section of the supermarket and see how many different noodles there are.

When preparing pasta for large groups of people, precook the noodles up to two days ahead, drain, rinse well, and toss with a little oil. Pack in individual plastic bags and refrigerate until ready to use. Bring several pots of water to a boil, place the cooked pasta in metal sieves, and cook individual portions by plunging them into the hot water for a few minutes. Drain and serve, offering a wide choice of toppings using the freshest ingredients. To permit guests to sample three or four dishes allow a total of 4 to 6 ounces of pasta per person at a pasta party. For a meal that includes other courses, allow 3 to 4 ounces of pasta per person. You are assured to please any crowd with a delightful panoply of pasta.

COOKING UDON AND SOBA NOODLES

Although you can cook Japanese noodles like Italian pasta, the method used in Japan is somewhat different. Unlike Italian pasta, which is made from semolina, Japanese noodles are made from wheat or buckwheat. As these noodles cook, the surface can easily become overdone with the center remaining undercooked.

The trick to cooking these noodles is to bring a pot of water to a boil, add the noodles, and when the water returns to the boil, add a cup of cold water. Each time the water returns to the boil, add another cup of cold water, until the noodles are done. Test for doneness by cutting into a single strand. It will be firm and tender when ready.

Drain immediately and rinse under cold running water to prevent the noodles from sticking together. Japanese noodles can be precooked and refrigerated until ready to use. Reheat by plunging into boiling water.

SOBA WITH SAUTÉED VEGETABLES

1 pound (450 g) eggplant (aubergine),
    preferably Japanese, cut into $\frac{1}{2}$-inch
    (1.3-cm) slices
Peanut oil
2 medium zucchini (courgettes), split
    and cut into $\frac{1}{2}$-inch (1.3-cm) slices
1 red bell pepper (capsicum), cut into
    $\frac{1}{3}$-inch (8-mm) rings
$\frac{1}{4}$ cup (55 g) white miso paste
2 tablespoons water
$\frac{1}{4}$ cup (60 ml) freshly squeezed
    orange juice
$\frac{1}{4}$ teaspoon cayenne
2 teaspoons umeboshi or balsamic vinegar
2 teaspoons grated orange zest
2 teaspoons coarsely ground black pepper
1 pound (450 g) soba noodles, cooked
    (page 173)
$\frac{1}{2}$ cup (120 ml) hot vegetable stock
2 scallions, thinly sliced

Umeboshi and miso accent the eggplant, red bell pepper, and zucchini in this flavorful dish.

Yield: 4 servings

If you are using large eggplant, cut the rounds in half.

Heat some oil in a large, heavy sauté pan set over medium-high heat. Working in batches, sauté the eggplant until golden brown on both sides, about 3 minutes per side. Sauté the zucchini. When it is browned, add the red pepper and eggplant, cover, and cook about 3 minutes, or until the vegetables are just soft.

Put the miso, water, orange juice, cayenne, umeboshi, zest, and black pepper in a small saucepan set over medium heat and cook, stirring, until heated through, about 3 minutes.

Divide the noodles among 4 plates. Moisten each portion with 2 tablespoons of the hot stock. Top with the sautéed vegetables and sauce, and sprinkle with scallion.

zucchini

UDON WITH WILD MUSHROOMS

4 ounces (115 g) mixed dried wild
   mushrooms (wood, morels, porcini,
   chanterelles, trumpet)
$^1/_2$ pound (230 g) white mushrooms, cut
   into $^1/_4$-inch (6-mm) slices
1 cup (250 ml) warm water
3 tablespoons olive oil
1 medium onion, peeled and cut into
   $^1/_4$-inch (6-mm) dice
4 cloves garlic, finely chopped
4 tablespoons ($^1/_2$ stick) (55 g) unsalted
   butter
3 tablespoons white miso paste
$^1/_2$ cup (55 g) ground walnuts
$^1/_2$ cup (120 ml) vegetable stock
1 tablespoon tamari or soy sauce
6 ounces (170 g) sunchokes, peeled and
   cut into $^1/_4$-inch (6-mm) slices
$^1/_2$ cup (55 g) freshly grated Parmesan
   cheese
1 pound (450 g) udon noodles, cooked
$^1/_4$ cup (10 g) chopped parsley

Lightly sautéed wild mushrooms are cooked in a rich walnut-Parmesan sauce, with crunchy Jerusalem artichokes, or sunchokes, adding their distinctive flavor.

Yield: 4 servings

Soak the mushrooms in the warm water for 30 minutes. Drain, reserving the liquid. Cut the mushrooms into $^1/_4$-inch (6-mm) slices, and strain the liquid through a cheesecloth-lined sieve or coffee filter.

Heat the oil in a large, heavy sauté pan set over medium-high heat and sauté the onion and garlic until soft but not browned.

Add the butter. When it melts, add the wild mushrooms and white mushrooms, and sauté 2 minutes.

Stir in the miso paste and ground walnuts, and cook 1 minute. Add the vegetable stock, mushroom-soaking liquid, and tamari. Cook 3 minutes, or until heated through. Add the sunchokes and cook 3 minutes more, stirring. Stir in the Parmesan and pour over the cooked noodles. Sprinkle with the parsley and serve.

UDON WITH VEGETABLES AND GADO-GADO SAUCE

4 large dried shiitake mushrooms

1 cup (250 ml) warm water

1 pound (450 g) string beans, cut into
    2-inch (5-cm) lengths

1 red bell pepper (capsicum), halved and
    cut into $^{1}/_{4}$-inch (6-mm) slices

1 green bell pepper (capsicum), halved
    and cut into $^{1}/_{4}$-inch (6-mm) slices

1 medium carrot, cut into julienne

2 tablespoons peanut or olive oil

1 tablespoon Asian sesame oil

8 ounces (230 g) firm tofu (soybean
    curd), rinsed and cut into 1-inch
    (2.5-cm) cubes

2 cups (170 g) bok choy, cut into
    $^{1}/_{2}$-inch (1.3-cm) slices

4 scallions, cut into 2-inch (5-cm) lengths

2 cups (4 ounces/115 g) bean sprouts

1 English (hothouse) cucumber, peeled,
    split, and sliced $^{1}/_{4}$-inch (6-mm) thick
    on the diagonal

1 pound (450 g) udon, cooked (page 173)

Gado-Gado Sauce (recipe follows)

$^{1}/_{4}$ cup (10 g) finely chopped cilantro
    (fresh coriander)

Gado-gado, a hot sauce of chili, peanuts, tamarind, and spices, is served throughout Indonesia over lightly steamed vegetables. This version combines the sauce with chewy udon noodles to make a delicious meal.

Yield: 6 servings

Soak the mushrooms in the water 30 minutes. Drain, reserving the liquid. Cut the mushrooms into $^{1}/_{4}$-inch (6-mm) strips, and strain the liquid through a cheesecloth-lined sieve or coffee filter.

Steam the string beans, red and green peppers, and carrots until tender but still crisp. Plunge into cold water to stop the cooking. Drain and set aside.

Heat the peanut and sesame oils in a wok or a large, heavy sauté pan set over high heat and cook the tofu, turning gently, on all sides 3 minutes. Transfer to paper towels (kitchen paper) to drain. Add the shiitake, bok choy, string beans, and bell peppers to the pan, and stir-fry 2 minutes. Add the scallion, bean sprouts, and cucumber, and stir-fry 30 seconds. Add the tofu, tossing gently, then add the cooked noodles and toss gently to mix. Top with Gado-Gado Sauce and sprinkle with the cilantro.

GADO-GADO SAUCE

2 tablespoons tamarind paste
¼ cup (60 ml) hot water
3 tablespoons vegetable oil
½ cup (55 g) finely chopped onion
2 cloves garlic, finely chopped
2 cups (500 ml) water
2 cups (450 g) smooth unsweetened
   peanut butter
3 tablespoons packed brown sugar
1 teaspoon red-pepper flakes
1-inch (2.5-cm) piece gingerroot, grated
1 teaspoon salt
4 cups (1 l) coconut milk

Soak the tamarind in the hot water 30 minutes. Strain, pressing on the pulp to extract the liquid. Discard the pulp, reserving the liquid.

Heat the oil in a medium, heavy saucepan set over medium-high heat and sauté the onions and garlic 5 minutes, or until soft. Add the water, raise the heat to high, and bring to a boil.

Add the peanut butter, sugar, red-pepper flakes, ginger, salt, tamarind-soaking liquid, and coconut milk. Reduce the heat and simmer 15 minutes.

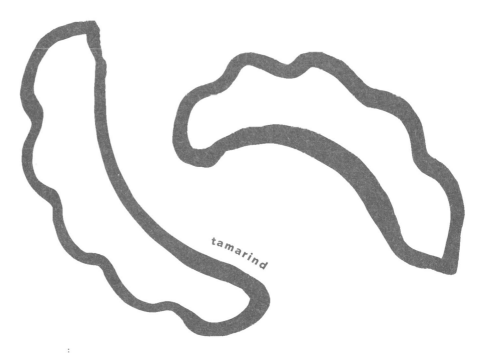

tamarind

MEXICAN FETTUCCINE WITH TOMATILLOS AND AVOCADO

Yield: 4 servings

½ cup (20 g) cilantro (fresh coriander)
¼ cup (10 g) flat-leaf parsley
3 cloves garlic, peeled
*4 scallions, cut into 1-inch (2.5-cm)
    lengths*
*2 jalapeño peppers, seeded and coarsely
    chopped*
8 ounces (230 g) tomatillos, quartered
¼ cup (60 ml) tequila
½ cup (120 ml) water
1 tablespoon vegetable oil
2 teaspoons ground cumin
1 tablespoon oregano
Salt and ground black pepper
*10 ounces (280 g) spinach fettuccine,
    cooked*
1 avocado
1 tablespoon freshly squeezed lime juice
Sour cream

Put the cilantro and parsley in a food processor and process until finely chopped. With the motor running, add the garlic and scallion and process 5 seconds. Add the jalapeño and process 5 seconds more. Transfer the mixture to a bowl.

Put the tomatillos in the food processor and pulse to chop. Add the tequila and water, and process until puréed.

Heat the oil in a medium sauté pan set over medium heat and sauté the jalapeño mixture until soft, about 3 minutes. Add the cumin, oregano, and tomatillo purée, season with salt and pepper, and simmer until slightly thickened, about 10 minutes. Add the cooked fettuccine and heat through.

Peel and pit the avocado. Cut the avocado in half lengthwise, cut each half into ¼-inch (6-mm) slices, and fan slices out. Sprinkle with the lime juice. Serve the fettuccine with the avocado fans and sour cream.

avocado

PASTA SHELLS WITH CITRUS-PEPPER SHRIMP SAUCE

4 cloves garlic, peeled
1 carrot, cut into 1-inch (2.5-cm) lengths
1 medium onion, quartered
34-ounce (960-g) can plum (egg)
    tomatoes, drained, 1/2 cup (120 ml)
    liquid reserved
1/4 cup (60 ml) olive oil
1 teaspoon red-pepper flakes
1 pound (450 g) medium shrimp
    (prawns), shelled, deveined, and split
1 teaspoon freshly squeezed lemon juice
1 teaspoon grated lemon zest
1 teaspoon freshly squeezed orange juice
1 teaspoon grated orange zest
Salt and ground black pepper
1 pound (450 g) small pasta shells, cooked
1/2 cup (25 g) tightly packed basil,
    finely chopped

This tasty sauce is trapped by the small pasta shells, making each mouthful filled with flavor.

Yield: 6 servings

Drop the garlic into a food processor with the motor running and process 10 seconds. Add the carrot and pulse 5 times. Add the onion and pulse 5 more times, or until finely chopped. Transfer the mixture to a bowl. Put the tomatoes in the processor and process until smooth, about 5 seconds.

Heat the oil in a large sauté pan set over medium heat, cover, and cook the vegetable mixture 5 minutes. Add the tomato purée, reserved tomato juice, and red-pepper flakes, and simmer 5 minutes. Add the shrimp and cook about 2 minutes more. Add the lemon juice and zest and orange juice and zest, and season with salt and pepper. Pour the sauce and basil over the shells and toss to mix.

FETTUCCINE WITH SHIITAKE-LOBSTER SAUCE

1/3 cup (80 ml) olive oil

2 pounds (900 g) small lobster tails

1 medium onion, peeled and quartered

6 cloves garlic, peeled

2 tablespoons grated gingerroot

1 medium carrot, cut into julienne

12 cherry tomatoes, quartered

1/4 teaspoon ground turmeric

1/4 teaspoon cayenne

2 cups (500 ml) dry white wine

Salt and ground black pepper

1/2 cup (120 ml) heavy (double) cream

1/2 cup (120 ml) sour cream

4 tablespoons (1/2 stick) (55 g) unsalted
   butter

1 pound (450 g) shiitake mushrooms,
   stems removed

1 1/2 pounds (675 g) fettuccine, cooked

Cilantro (fresh coriander) sprigs
   for garnish

Hiding in cracks and under rocky crevices in the reefs, the clawless Hawaiian spiny lobster with its big head and little tail has a meat that is firm, tender, and very sweet. Much smaller than its European and Maine relatives, the spiny lobster grows to just three or four pounds. The crustacean is also a favorite meal of the moray eel, and many divers relate tales of morays fighting them for their catch by trying to wrench the lobster out of their thickly gloved hands.

Yield: 6 servings

Heat the oil in a large, heavy sauté pan set over medium heat and cook the lobster tails in their shells, stirring and turning, about 6 minutes. Remove with a slotted spoon.

Add the onion, 4 of the garlic cloves, the ginger, and carrots, and cook, stirring, 1 minute. Add the tomatoes, turmeric, cayenne, and 1 1/2 cups (375 ml) of the wine. Season with salt, cover, and cook 10 minutes, stirring occasionally. Add the heavy cream, sour cream, and the remaining 1/2 cup (120 ml) wine, cover, and cook 15 minutes more. Strain the sauce, extracting as much liquid as possible and discarding the solids.

Meanwhile, remove the lobster meat from the shells and cut into bite-size pieces.

Finely chop the remaining 2 cloves garlic. Heat the butter in a large sauté pan set over low heat. Add the garlic and mushrooms, season with salt and pepper, and cook 5 minutes. Add the lobster meat and the sauce, and cook 5 minutes more.

Put the fettuccine in a large bowl, add the sauce, and toss. Garnish with cilantro sprigs.

PASTA WITH SMOKED SALMON AND WATERCRESS

1 tablespoon unsalted butter

1 medium red onion, coarsely chopped

2 cups (500 ml) heavy (double) cream

2 teaspoons coarsely ground black pepper

12 ounces (340 g) fettuccine, cooked,
   ¼ cup (60 ml) cooking liquid
   reserved

1 bunch watercress (6 ounces/170 g),
   trimmed and finely chopped

6 ounces (170 g) smoked salmon cut into
   ¼-inch (6-mm) dice

Grated zest of 1 lime

Watercress is widely eaten throughout the islands and appears frequently in many Asian dishes. Some of the best watercress comes from the island of Oahu and has large, juicy stems and peppery leaves.

Yield: 4 servings

Heat the butter in a medium sauté pan set over low heat and cook the onions until softened, about 5 minutes. Remove the onion and add the cream and pepper to the pan. Cook until reduced to 1½ cups (375 ml), about 8 minutes. In a large bowl, toss the fettuccine with the reserved cooking liquid, reduced cream, watercress, onion, and salmon. Sprinkle with lime zest and serve.

FRESH-HERB PASTA

3 tablespoons extra-virgin olive oil

2 medium onions, cut into $^1/_4$-inch
   (6-mm) dice

6 cloves garlic, finely chopped

1 red bell pepper (capsicum), cut into
   $^1/_4$-inch (6-mm) squares

1 green bell pepper (capsicum), cut into
   $^1/_4$-inch (6-mm) squares

$^1/_2$ pound (230 g) white mushrooms,
   cut into $^1/_4$-inch (6-mm) dice

$^1/_2$ pound (230 g) plum (egg) tomatoes,
   peeled, seeded, and cut into $^1/_4$-inch
   (6-mm) dice

$^1/_2$ cup (75 g) kalamata olives, pitted
   and finely chopped

$^1/_4$ cup (40 g) capers

1 cup (250 ml) vegetable stock

$^1/_3$ cup (80 ml) dry white wine

$^1/_4$ cup (10 g) finely chopped mixed fresh
   herbs, such as oregano, basil, thyme,
   rosemary, and parsley

Salt and pepper

1 pound (450 g) linguini or fettuccine,
   cooked

Although this dish is more Mediterranean than Pacific Rim, I have included it because of its bright tropical colors and freshness. All the ingredients can be prepared well in advance, covered tightly in separate bowls, and refrigerated, then cooked just minutes before serving.

Yield: 4 servings

Heat the oil in a large, heavy sauté pan set over medium-high heat and sauté the onions and garlic 2 minutes, or until soft. Add the red and green bell peppers and cook 1 minute. Add the mushrooms, tomatoes, olives, and capers and cook 2 minutes more, stirring.

Add the stock and wine, and cook until the liquid is hot. Stir in the herbs and season with salt and pepper. Reduce the heat and simmer 5 minutes more. Pour the sauce over the hot pasta and serve.

PAN-FRIED NOODLES

8 ounces (230 g) Chinese cellophane
noodles
¹/₄ cup (60 ml) peanut oil

Noodles served this way make a great base for sautés, stir-fries, or any dish with a rich sauce.

Yield: 4 servings

Cook the noodles in lightly salted boiling water until al dente. Drain in a colander and rinse under cold water.

Lightly oil 4 small plates. Divide the noodles among the plates, flattening and spreading them out to form a disc. Let sit about 2 hours, turning the discs once.

Heat the oil in a large, heavy sauté pan set over medium-high heat. Slide one of the noodle discs carefully off the plate into the hot oil. Fry until golden, turn, and brown the other side, about 3 minutes per side. Transfer to paper towels (kitchen paper) to drain. Repeat with the remaining discs. Keep warm in a low oven until ready to serve.

SALSAS, CHUTNEYS, AND SAUCES

WITH bright, enticing, colorful combinations that are much healthier than the rich cream sauces that have accompanied our food in the past, salsa is a welcome addition to our diet. Served in bowls with tortilla chips as an appetizer, spooned into a chilled soup like Tropical Gazpacho (page 67), or used in an enticing combination with Seared Marinated Swordfish (page 135), salsa can bring vibrancy to any meal.

Moving away from the familiar red salsa made with tomato, onion, and chilies, and green salsa, made with tomatillos and chilies, we now find ourselves topping broiled fish, lamb kebabs, chicken skewers, quesadillas, curries, seafood stews, and just about every other kind of dish with exotic and intriguing salsas. We are dicing up pineapple, papaya, coconut, jícama, and mango and combining them with jalapeño, serrano, and chipotle chilies. We're adding fresh herbs, squeezing in fresh lime, orange, lemon, or tangerine juice, adding grated ginger, garlic, and spices, and spooning salsas over all sorts of grilled, baked, stewed, roasted, and curried dishes.

Prepare all your ingredients in advance. Dice, chop, grate, and slice your ingredients, seal them tightly in individual containers, and refrigerate. Then, about 15 minutes before you are ready to eat, toss them together and allow the flavors to develop before serving. The only rule to preparing salsa is that all the ingredients be very fresh.

Apart from the dynamic flavors and the fact that they take almost no time to prepare, other merits of salsa are that they contain virtually no fat and are easily mixed and matched to suit your own tastes.

Start by trying some of these salsa recipes. Enjoy the refreshing way Sesame-Ginger-Crusted Ahi (page 131) is brought to life topped with Mango-Pineapple Salsa (page 188). Or cool down Tropical Spicy Chicken (page 144) with fragrant Papaya-Mango-Mint Salsa (page 188). Chicken Satay (page 149) is transformed when served with rice mounded with Asian Salsa (page 189): the fresh flavors of the salsa contrast nicely with the dense peanut sauce.

Even though chutneys take longer to prepare, you can make the recipes in large batches, pour the hot mixture into sterilized jars, and store them, refrigerated, indefinitely, therefore always having some on hand. Grilled Ginger Chicken (page 155) or a simple roast duck is perfect with Pineapple Chutney (page 193). For a flavorful East-meets-West meal, team Chicken in Sun-Dried-Tomato Sauce (page 145) with Bamboo Shoot

Pickle (page 195). Banana-Raisin Chutney (page 192) goes wonderfully with curries, plain grilled fish, or barbecued chicken.

Consider charring or roasting some of the ingredients. Roast chilies by placing them over a gas flame on the stove or directly on a hot grill, turning frequently to allow the skin to char. When the skin is blackened, place the hot chilies in a paper or plastic bag, seal, and allow them to steam for about 10 minutes. The skin can then easily be removed by holding the chilies under running cool water. Then dice and use in the recipe as directed. The resulting flavors will impart a depth and smoky character to the salsa.

Tomatoes and tomatillos can be treated much the same way: char as you would chilies, though without peeling, and dice. You may also want to experiment with roasting whole unpeeled garlic. Place in a 400°F (200°C) oven for about 20 minutes, cool, then squeeze the softened pulp from the skins.

Grilling some of the fruits or vegetables is another way to experiment. The roasted kernels of fresh corn grilled on the cob are a tasty addition to salsa. Pineapples, mangoes, and papayas may all be grilled to add a new dimension of taste to your salsa. Be careful not to overcook fruit—grill just enough to char the outside and keep the inside crisp and intact. Try these recipes, then create your own unique combinations.

PAPAYA·MANGO·MINT SALSA

Yield: 2 1/2 cups

1 pound (450 g) firm, ripe papaya
    (pawpaw), cut into 1/4-inch
    (6-mm) dice
1 firm, ripe mango, cut into 1/4-inch
    (6-mm) dice
1/2 red onion, cut into 1/4-inch
    (6-mm) dice
1/2 cup (20 g) mint, chopped
1/2 cup (120 ml) freshly squeezed
    lime juice
1/4 cup (60 ml) vegetable oil
Salt to taste

Toss all the ingredients in a large, nonreactive mixing bowl.

MANGO·PINEAPPLE SALSA

Yield: 2 cups

1/2 medium Maui or Vidalia (sweet)
    onion, coarsely chopped
2 cloves garlic, peeled
1 firm, ripe mango, coarsely chopped
1/2 pineapple, cut into 1-inch (2.5-cm)
    chunks
1/2 cup (20 g) loosely packed cilantro
    (fresh coriander)
1 tablespoon freshly squeezed lime juice
1 teaspoon salt
1 teaspoon ground black pepper

Put all the ingredients in a food processor, pulse several times, then process until coarsely chopped and well blended.

ASIAN SALSA

6 dried black mushrooms

2 medium tomatoes, seeded and
    coarsely chopped

1 jícama (about 5 ounces/140 g),
    peeled and coarsely chopped

1 cup (115 g) thinly sliced scallion

1/2 cup (20 g) loosely packed cilantro
    (fresh coriander)

3 cloves garlic, peeled

2-inch (5-cm) piece gingerroot, grated

2 tablespoons mirin

2 tablespoons Asian sesame oil

1 tablespoon vegetable oil

1 1/2 teaspoons honey

1 teaspoon chili oil or 1 teaspoon cayenne

1 teaspoon salt

Yield: 1 1/2 cups

Soak the mushrooms in warm water for 30 minutes. Drain, remove and discard the stems, and coarsely chop. Put all the ingredients in a food processor, pulse, then process 2 seconds to blend.

TROPICAL·FRUIT SALSA

1 medium red onion, cut into 8 wedges

$^1/_2$ green bell pepper (capsicum),
    coarsely chopped

$^1/_2$ red bell pepper (capsicum),
    coarsely chopped

1 small green chili pepper, seeded
    and chopped

1 tablespoon freshly squeezed lime juice

$^1/_2$ cup (20 g) loosely packed cilantro
    (fresh coriander)

1 teaspoon salt

1 teaspoon ground black pepper

1 teaspoon cayenne

2 medium tomatoes

$^1/_2$ pineapple, cut into 1-inch (2.5-cm)
    chunks

$^1/_2$ medium ripe papaya (pawpaw),
    cut into 1-inch (2.5-cm) chunks

1 large or two small oranges, sectioned,
    membranes removed

2 small star fruit (carambolas),
    coarsely chopped

Yield: 3 cups

Put the onion, green and red bell peppers, chili pepper, lime juice, cilantro, salt, pepper, and cayenne in a food processor and pulse 5 times. Transfer to a large, nonreactive mixing bowl. Put the tomato, pineapple, papaya, orange, and star fruit in the processor, pulse 5 times, then process 2 seconds to blend. Transfer to the mixing bowl and stir gently to mix well.

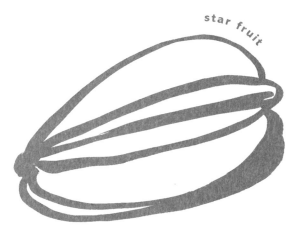

star fruit

TOMATO-GINGER SALSA

Yield: 1 ¹/₂ cups

1 medium red onion, coarsely chopped

2 medium tomatoes, seeded and coarsely
   chopped

¹/₂ green bell pepper (capsicum),
   coarsely chopped

1-inch (2.5-cm) piece gingerroot, grated

¹/₄ cup (10 g) cilantro (fresh coriander)

2 tablespoons freshly squeezed lime juice

1 tablespoon balsamic vinegar

2 teaspoons chili oil or 1 teaspoon cayenne

1 teaspoon salt

1 teaspoon ground black pepper

Put all the ingredients in a food processor. Pulse 8 times, then process 2 seconds to blend.

COCONUT-MANGO SALSA

Yield: 2 cups

1 red onion, coarsely chopped

2 cloves garlic, peeled

3 large firm ripe mangoes, coarsely
   chopped

2-inch (5-cm) piece gingerroot, grated

2 tablespoons dark rum

1 tablespoon freshly squeezed lime juice

1 teaspoon sugar

¹/₂ cup (20 g) loosely packed cilantro
   (fresh coriander)

¹/₂ cup (120 ml) coconut milk

¹/₂ cup (45 g) grated coconut

Put the onion, garlic, mango, and ginger in a food processor and pulse 5 times. Add the rum, lime juice, sugar, and cilantro and pulse 3 times. Add the coconut milk and grated coconut, pulse, then process 3 seconds.

PAPAYA-PINEAPPLE SALSA

Yield: 2 cups

1/2 medium onion, coarsely chopped
2 cloves garlic, peeled
1 medium firm ripe papaya (pawpaw),
*   cut into 1-inch (2.5-cm) chunks*
1/2 pineapple, cut into 1-inch (2.5-cm)
*   chunks*
1/2 cup (20 g) loosely packed basil
1/4 cup (10 g) loosely packed cilantro
*   (fresh coriander)*
1 tablespoon freshly squeezed lime juice
1 teaspoon salt
1 teaspoon ground black pepper

Put all the ingredients in a food processor and pulse until evenly chopped, then process 2 seconds to blend.

BANANA-RAISIN CHUTNEY

Yield: 4 cups

1 lemon
3 cloves garlic, finely chopped
6 cups (900 g) chopped firm banana,
*   preferably apple or strawberry*
*   bananas*
2 1/2 cups (365 g) firmly packed
*   brown sugar*
2 cups (300 g) golden raisins (sultanas)
1/2 cup (120 g) grated gingerroot
2 teaspoons salt
1 teaspoon cayenne
2 1/2 cups (625 ml) cider vinegar
2 red bell peppers (capsicums), cut into
*   1/2-inch (1.3-cm) squares*

Chop the lemon, peel and all, and pick out the seeds. Put all the ingredients in a large saucepan set over medium-low heat and simmer until the fruit is tender.

PINEAPPLE CHUTNEY

1 cup (200 g) granulated sugar

1 cup (155 g) firmly packed light-brown
sugar

$^3/_4$ cup (180 ml) Japanese rice vinegar

1 small onion, thinly sliced

$^1/_2$ cup (100 g) preserved or candied
gingerroot

5 cloves garlic, thinly sliced

1 cup (140 g) raisins

2 teaspoons mustard seed

$1^1/_2$ teaspoons salt

1 teaspoon red-pepper flakes

1 large red bell pepper (capsicum),
cut into julienne

1 red chili pepper, seeded and finely
chopped

1 large pineapple, cut into $^3/_4$ inch
(2-cm) chunks

This chutney is perfect served with grilled chicken or duck.

Yield: 3 cups (675 g)

Put the granulated sugar, brown sugar, and vinegar in a 4-quart (4-l) saucepan set over medium heat and cook until the sugar has dissolved and the mixture begins to boil. Add the onion, ginger, garlic, raisins, mustard seed, salt, and red-pepper flakes and stir well. Add the red bell pepper, chili pepper, and pineapple.

Reduce the heat and simmer, stirring often, about $1^1/_2$ hours, or until the mixture thickens.

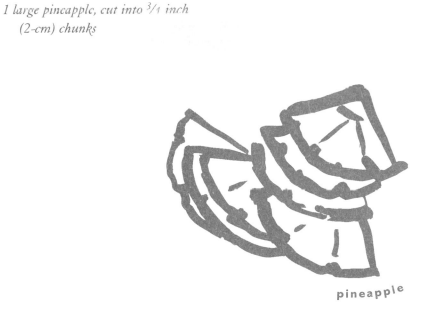

pineapple

MANGO CHUTNEY

10 cups (1.4 kg) sliced green to half-ripe
   mangoes
2 tablespoons kosher salt
2 cups (500 ml) cider vinegar
4 cups (800 g) Demerara or turbinado or
   brown sugar
2 red onions, cut into 8 wedges and
   separated
4 cloves garlic, finely chopped
4-inch (10-cm) piece gingerroot, finely
   chopped
3 red chilies, seeded and finely chopped
1 cup (140 g) raw cashew nuts
Zest of 1 orange, cut into julienne

Yield: 6 cups

Toss the mango with the salt and let stand at least 4 hours or overnight. Rinse with cold water and drain well.

    Put the vinegar and sugar in a large, heavy saucepan, bring to a boil, stirring, then reduce the heat and simmer 30 minutes.

    Add the mango, onion, garlic, ginger, chilies, nuts, and zest, and simmer 1 hour, stirring occasionally, until the fruit is tender and the mixture is thick.

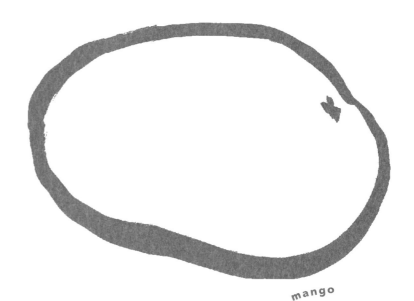

mango

BAMBOO SHOOT PICKLE

Yield: 4 to 6 cups

2 cloves garlic, peeled
½ ounce (15 g) (6 to 8) macadamia nuts
1 teaspoon sugar
1 teaspoon ground coriander
¼ teaspoon turmeric
½ teaspoon salt
2 tablespoons water
1 tablespoon vegetable oil
2 8-ounce (230-g) cans sliced bamboo
    shoots, drained
1 medium jalapeño pepper, seeded and
    finely chopped
¼ teaspoon red-pepper flakes
½ onion, cut in quarters
3-inch (7.5-cm) piece lemon grass,
    finely chopped, or grated zest of
    ¼ lime and ¼ lemon
3 tablespoons Japanese rice vinegar
½ teaspoon grated gingerroot

With the motor running, drop the garlic, nuts, and sugar in a food processor and process 10 seconds, or until finely chopped. Add the coriander, turmeric, salt, and water, and process to a paste, about 5 seconds, stopping to scrape down the sides of the bowl as necessary.

Heat the oil in a medium saucepan set over medium heat and cook the mixture, stirring, 2 minutes. Add the bamboo shoots, jalapeño, red-pepper flakes, onion, lemon grass or lime and lemon zests, vinegar, and ginger, and cook 4 minutes. Allow to cool, then refrigerate at least 4 hours. Bring to room temperature before serving.

JÍCAMA AND ONION PICKLE

4 cloves garlic, peeled

1 ounce (30 g) (12 to 16) macadamia nuts

1 teaspoon firmly packed brown sugar

2 teaspoons ground coriander

1 teaspoon ground dried turmeric or
    2 teaspoons grated fresh

1 teaspoon salt

2 tablespoons cold water

1 tablespoon vegetable oil

1 medium onion, cut into 8 wedges
    and separated

1 pound (450 g) jícama, peeled,
    quartered, and thinly sliced

1 medium red bell pepper (capsicum),
    halved and thinly sliced

1 tablespoon grated gingerroot

1/2 teaspoon red-pepper flakes

Zest of 1/4 lemon, cut into julienne

Zest of 1/4 lime, cut into julienne

3 tablespoons cider vinegar

Turmeric gives this dish its bright festive color. A rhizome (like ginger), turmeric is more familiar to most cooks in its dried and powdered form. It is the bright orange-yellow coloring agent used in commercial curry powders. In its fresh form, the knobby, brown-skinned "roots" are peeled and either grated or finely chopped. Use 2 teaspoons grated fresh turmeric to replace 1 teaspoon powdered turmeric.

Yield: 1 1/2 cups

With the motor running, drop the garlic and nuts into a food processor and process until finely chopped. Add the sugar, coriander, turmeric, salt, and water, and process to a paste, stopping to scrape down the sides of the bowl as necessary.

Heat the oil in a large, heavy saucepan set over medium heat and cook the mixture, stirring, 2 minutes. Add the onion, jícama, bell pepper, ginger, red-pepper flakes, lemon and lime zests, and vinegar, and cook 5 minutes more. Serve at room temperature.

jicama

GUACAMOLE

Yield: 2 cups

4 cloves garlic, peeled

1 medium Maui or Vidalia (sweet)
   onion, quartered

1 small red bell pepper (capsicum),
   coarsely chopped

1 small jalapeño pepper, seeded and
   coarsely chopped

2 tablespoons cilantro (fresh coriander)

1/2 teaspoon cayenne

2 medium ripe avocados, coarsely chopped

Juice of 1 lime

Salt and pepper to taste

With the motor running, drop the garlic into the food processor. Add the onion, bell pepper, and jalapeño, and pulse 5 times. Add the cilantro and cayenne, and pulse. Add the avocado, lime juice, salt, and pepper, and pulse to coarsely blend. Refrigerate until ready to use.

RED PEPPER AND MACADAMIA NUT PESTO

Yield: 1 cup

2 red bell peppers (capsicums), peeled,
   seeded, and coarsely chopped

3 cloves garlic, coarsely chopped

1/4 cup (4 tablespoons) coarsely chopped
   macadamia nuts

1/2 teaspoon paprika

1 teaspoon freshly squeezed lime juice

1 teaspoon salt

1/4 cup (60 ml) macadamia nut or
   vegetable oil

Put the bell pepper and garlic in a food processor, and pulse and process until smooth. Add the nuts, paprika, lime juice, and salt, and process to blend. With the motor running, add the oil in a steady stream and process until incorporated.

HUMMUS

15-ounce (420-g) can chickpeas, drained,
   liquid reserved
3 cloves garlic
1/2 cup (115 g) tahini
2 teaspoons freshly squeezed lemon juice
Salt and ground black pepper

Yield: 1 1/2 cups

Put the chickpeas and garlic in a food processor, pulse, then process to finely chop, stopping to scrape down the sides of the bowl as necessary. Add 1/2 cup (60 ml) of the reserved liquid and pulse. Add the tahini and lemon juice, and process until smooth. Season with salt and pepper.

PAPAYA-BASIL PURÉE

1 pound (450 g) ripe papaya (pawpaw),
   cut into 2-inch (5-cm) chunks
1/2 cup (25 g) tightly packed basil
1/2 cup (120 ml) coconut milk
Juice of 1 lime
Salt and pepper

Yield: 1 1/2 cups

Put the papaya and basil in a food processor and process until smooth. Add the coconut milk and lime juice, season with salt and pepper, and process until well blended.

YOGURT-CUCUMBER SAUCE

Yield: 2¹/4 cups

1 medium cucumber, grated
2 teaspoons ground coriander
Salt to taste
2 cups (450 g) plain yogurt

Combine all the ingredients and stir gently to mix.

CILANTRO-LIME HOLLANDAISE

Yield: ³/4 cup

2 large egg yolks
¹/4 teaspoon salt
1 tablespoon finely chopped cilantro
    (fresh coriander)
Juice of ¹/2 lime
8 tablespoons (1 stick) (115 g) unsalted
    butter, melted

Put the egg yolks, salt, cilantro, and lime juice in a blender. With the motor running, add the hot butter in a steady stream and blend until incorporated, about 20 seconds. Serve immediately.

DESSERTS

As a result of so many nationalities living side by side in a relatively small space, feasts observed by each group often overflow into the mainstream. Everybody gets to observe the holidays peculiar to his or her own nationality and also gets to enjoy the festivities of the other groups. What all these feasts have in common is that they are celebrated with an array of sweets.

For Polynesians celebration feasts include weddings, the completion of a house, the launching of a new canoe, and the first birthday of a child. At these traditional feasts dessert would most likely be haupia (page 220), a firm coconut pudding. These occasions inspired my Fresh Tropical Fruit Galette with Macadamia-Nut Paste (page 221), which uses typical Hawaiian ingredients.

On Chinese New Year, in which just about everybody in the community participates, many varieties of candied fruits and nuts are served, and also a steamed pudding made from rice flour and brown sugar. Also served at New Year's is a puffed-rice candy soaked in syrup and combined with peanuts and sesame seeds, which is cut into diamond-shaped pieces. Another Chinese feast is the moon festival, at which small round cakes with sweet red or black bean paste are eaten. Coconut, gingerroot, lotus seeds, and other fruits and vegetables are candied in sugar syrup, and peanuts and sesame seeds are cooked with sugar to make brittle.

Japanese dessert offerings include the very popular mochi, a glutinous rice that is boiled, pounded, sweetened, and formed into balls. These are served at New Year's and on May 5, which is Boys Day. On Boys Day, Japanese families erect displays of flying carp fastened to bamboo poles in front of their houses, with the number of carp telling the number of sons in the family. On this day mochi rice is wrapped in bamboo leaves, steamed or boiled, and served hot with a mixture of soybean flour, sugar, and salt. Another cake made with mochi is shaped into balls and filled with azuki bean paste.

The Koreans celebrate New Year's, weddings, and birthdays, and, like the Chinese, the first and sixty-first birthdays are cause for elaborate celebrations. Nuts and glutinous-rice cakes are eaten on these occasions, as is a dessert called yaksik, made with dates or persimmons, brown sugar, shoyu, sesame oil, and pine nuts combined with glutinous rice.

The Portuguese, who are Catholics, celebrate many of the holidays associated with religious festivals. Their contributions include sweet rice puddings, malasadas (a type of doughnut), bread prepared with honey and almonds, and sponge cakes served with honey or lemon syrup. Christmas, Shrove Tuesday, and Easter are the important holidays.

For Filipinos the important holidays are political: Rizal Day, on December 30, and Commonwealth Day, on November 15. Religious feast days include christenings, weddings, and funerals. On these occasions candies are prepared from fruit and shredded coconut. Flan served with caramel syrup is very popular, as is pumpkin cooked with coconut milk to form a custard and a pudding of bananas and sweet potatoes or taro, sweetened and thickened with rice flour. Many of the cakes are deep-fried, as are bananas rolled in a batter made of rice flour served with chocolate. My interpretation of this dish is Banana Spring Rolls filled with chocolate mousse and almond cream (page 206).

New Year's Day is a huge celebration for the Thais, who celebrate it in the spring and call it Sonkran. Part of the festival includes the un-aware being drenched with water by fleet-footed children, who quickly run away, laughing. This is an adaptation of the ritual whereby Thais traditionally bathed their elders with holy water to show respect.

From Indonesia and Southeast Asia come desserts with various combinations of coconut, fruit, sugar, tamarind, and sweet rice. A zesty Indonesian mixture is Sweet-and-Hot Tropical Fruit Salad (page 219). Other desserts include tapioca pudding served cold and usually made with coconut milk that has pieces of diced fruit such as mango, papaya, or banana mixed in (page 218).

Many of the desserts presented here are based on traditional recipes. For example, Mile-High Meringue Tart (page 216), with lime and macadamia nut as the predominant flavors, is a tropical spinoff of lemon meringue pie. Passion Bars (page 205) are a variation of lemon bars, using passion fruit purée instead of lemon.

Here I would like to add an additional note on passion fruit, as it can be used to replace lemon or orange flavors in many desserts, giving commonplace desserts a wonderful tropical kick. Passion fruit, known in Hawaii as lilikoi, is a plump, round, often wrinkled purplish-brown or yellow-green humble-looking fruit. Tear open the skin, though, and an intense, exquisite aroma will pervade the air.

Some of these recipes may at first glance seem a little daunting, but with patience any cook can achieve wonderful results. The recipes are for the most part easily made well in advance, with last-minute touches added just before serving.

PASSION BARS

⅓ cup (45 g) macadamia nuts
Zest of 1 lemon
Zest of ½ orange
½ cup (70 g) all-purpose (plain) flour
¼ cup (45 g) powdered (icing) sugar
5 tablespoons (75 g) unsalted butter,
*   chilled and cut into 5 pieces*
¾ cup (150 g) granulated sugar
½ teaspoon baking powder
Pinch salt
2 large eggs, lightly beaten
1½ teaspoons freshly squeezed
*   lemon juice*
2 tablespoons passion fruit nectar

An island variation of lemon bars, these are made with a lilikoi, or passion fruit, filling covering a rich macadamia-nut short crust.

Yield: 12 bars

Preheat the oven to 400°F (200°C). Put the macadamia nuts, half the lemon and orange zests, the flour, powdered sugar, and butter in a food processor and process until the mixture resembles coarse crumbs, about 15 seconds. Press the mixture onto the bottom of an ungreased 8-inch- (20-cm-) square cake pan and bake until firm and lightly colored, about 15 minutes.

Put the granulated sugar, baking powder, salt, and remaining half of the lemon and orange zests in the food processor and process 1 minute. Add the eggs, lemon juice, and passion fruit nectar and process until combined, about 5 seconds. Pour the mixture over the crust and bake until set, about 15 minutes. Allow to cool and cut into 12 bars.

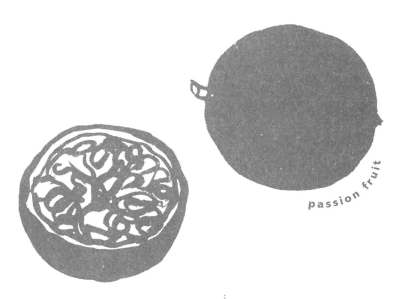

passion fruit

BANANA SPRING ROLLS

THE CHOCOLATE MOUSSE

4 ounces (115 g) unsweetened chocolate

²/₃ cup (140 g) sugar

¹/₄ cup (60 ml) water

3 large eggs, separated, at room
    temperature

¹/₄ teaspoon cream of tartar

2 teaspoons vanilla extract

THE ALMOND PASTE

¹/₄ cup (30 g) blanched almonds

¹/₄ cup (50 g) sugar

2 tablespoons unsalted butter, at room
    temperature

1 medium egg

¹/₂ teaspoon almond extract

THE BANANAS

6 firm ripe bananas

2 sheets filo pastry

3 tablespoons unsalted butter, melted

Vegetable oil for deep-frying

Bananas are hollowed out, filled with a rich chocolate mousse and almond cream, wrapped in thin pastry, and deep-fried. This dessert makes a sensational and elegant finale to any meal.

Yield: 6 servings

Break the chocolate into pieces, and put it in a food processor. Pulse a few times, then process until finely chopped, about 1 minute. Leave it in the bowl. Put ¹/₃ cup (70 g) of the sugar and the water in a small saucepan and bring to a boil. With the motor running, pour the boiling syrup through the feed tube and process until smooth. Leave it in the bowl. With an electric mixer, beat the egg whites with the cream of tartar until firm. Gradually add the remaining ¹/₃ cup (70 g) sugar, beating until stiff peaks form. Add the egg yolks and vanilla to the cooled chocolate mixture in the food processor and pulse until incorporated, stopping to scrape down the sides of the bowl. Add half the egg whites, pulse a few times, and transfer to a large bowl. Gently fold in the remaining egg whites. Refrigerate at least 3 hours, or until firm.

Clean the food processor.

Process the almonds and sugar until finely ground. Add the butter and pulse 4 times. Add the egg and almond extract, and process about 15 seconds, or until smooth. Refrigerate until ready to use.

Peel the bananas, split them, and hollow them out with a melon baller to form a channel, leaving the ends intact. Fill one half of each banana with chocolate mousse and the other half with almond paste, leveling it and scraping off the excess. Place the two halves together to re-form the banana.

BANANA SPRING ROLLS *(continued)*

Place one sheet of filo on a work surface. Brush with melted butter, then place the second sheet over the first, and brush with butter. Cut the double sheet in half lengthwise, then in thirds crosswise to make 6 rectangles. Place a filled banana in the center of one rectangle, fold the dough over the banana, and roll the banana up in the dough, tucking in the sides. (It should resemble a spring roll.) Brush the edge of the filo with butter to seal. Repeat with the remaining bananas. (The recipe can be made ahead to this point, and the rolls wrapped in plastic wrap [cling film] and refrigerated.)

Heat the oil and deep-fry the bananas until golden and crisp, turning frequently to avoid burning. Place on paper towels (kitchen paper) to drain.

Spoon the remaining mousse to one side of 6 plates. Cut each spring roll in half on a sharp diagonal. Place two halves on each plate, one standing upright and the other lying down on the opposite side of the mousse. Serve immediately.

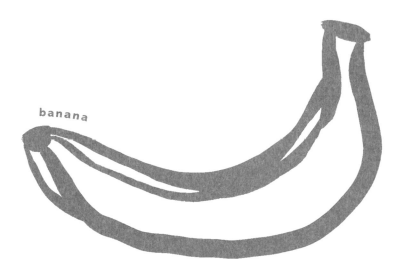

banana

GINGER-CINNAMON CANOES WITH PIÑA COLADA GRANITA

Vegetable oil for greasing pan
2-inch (5-cm) piece gingerroot, grated
8 tablespoons (1 stick) (115 g) unsalted
*   butter*
²⁄₃ cup (140 g) sugar
¹⁄₄ cup (60 ml) honey
²⁄₃ cup (95 g) all-purpose (plain) flour
2 teaspoons ground ginger
2 teaspoons ground cinnamon
Piña Colada Granita (recipe follows)
1 cup dried shredded coconut, toasted

Lacy canoes float by filled with icy-fresh piña colada granita. This is a fun dessert to serve around the pool on a hot summer evening.

Yield: 8 canoes

Preheat the oven to 400°F (200°C) and lightly oil a large baking sheet.

Squeeze the grated ginger to extract the juice; there should be 2 teaspoons. Discard the pulp.

Put the butter, sugar, and honey in a small saucepan set over medium-high heat and cook until the butter melts. Remove from the heat and stir in the flour, ginger juice, ground ginger, and cinnamon.

Place the mixture by ¼-cupfuls on the prepared baking sheet spaced well apart. With the back of a wet spoon spread the mixture to form rectangles with rounded ends about 5½ × 3 inches (14 × 7.5 cm) large. Bake 7 minutes, or until dark golden and well spread out.

Allow to cool slightly, then carefully peel from the baking sheet. Let cool a few minutes draped over a rolling pin or other cylindrical shape. When still slightly warm and a bit soft, pinch the ends together to form a canoe shape. When completely cool, pack in an airtight container until ready to use.

To assemble the canoes, place 2 or 3 scoops of the granita in each canoe and sprinkle with coconut.

PIÑA COLADA GRANITA

2¹/₂ cups (450 g) pineapple, cut into
   ¹/₂-inch (1.3 cm) cubes
12-ounce (340-ml) can cream of coconut
¹/₂ cup (120 ml) freshly squeezed
   lime juice
¹/₂ cup (120 ml) freshly squeezed orange
   juice
3 tablespoons dark rum
2 tablespoons Triple Sec or other
   orange-flavored liqueur

Yield: 1 ¹/₂ quarts

Working in batches, process the pineapple in a food processor for
15 seconds. Transfer to a large bowl. Stir in the cream of coconut,
lime juice, orange juice, rum, and Triple Sec. Cover with plastic
wrap (cling film) and place in the freezer overnight.

Working in batches, pulse the frozen mixture in a food
processor 10 times, then process until smooth, about 90 seconds.
Cover and freeze 2 hours, or until firm.

pineapple

DESSERTS

COCONUT FLORENTINES

8 tablespoons (1 stick) (115 g) unsalted
    butter plus more for buttering pan
1 cup (170 g) powdered (icing) sugar
1/2 cup (120 ml) heavy (double) cream
1/2 cup (70 g) all-purpose (plain) flour
1 teaspoon vanilla extract
1/2 cup (45 g) shredded coconut
1/2 cup (55 g) sliced almonds
2 teaspoons freshly squeezed lemon juice
8 ounces (230 g) semisweet (dark)
    chocolate
1/4 cup (60 ml) boiling water

I find the combination of coconut, orange, and chocolate irresistible. Serve these delicate cookies with vanilla ice cream.

Yield: 3 dozen cookies

Preheat the oven to 350°F (175°C) and line 2 baking sheets with lightly buttered parchment paper or foil.

Put the butter and cream in small saucepan set over medium-low heat. When the butter melts, stir in the flour. Remove from the heat and add the coconut mixture, almonds, and lemon juice. Mix well, then allow to cool.

Drop by teaspoonfuls onto the cookie sheets, about 2 inches (5 cm) apart. Bake in the lower third of the oven 10 minutes, or until the edges are browned. Invert the cookies onto wax paper and allow to cool completely.

Break the chocolate into pieces and place in the food processor. Pulse 6 to 8 times, then process 1 minute, or until finely chopped. With the motor running, pour the hot water through the feed tube. Process 10 seconds more, or until the chocolate is completely melted.

Using a spatula dipped in hot water, spread the chocolate thinly over one side of each cookie. Let cool at least 3 hours before serving. The cookies can be stored in an airtight container and refrigerated.

CANDIED ORANGE PEEL

Butter for greasing pan
2 navel oranges
1 cup (200 g) sugar
2/3 cup (160 ml) water

Butter a baking sheet. With a sharp knife or a vegetable peeler, peel the oranges, removing only the orange-colored zest. Put the zest in a food processor with 1/2 cup (100 g) of the sugar and process until the peel is coarsely chopped. Transfer the mixture to a medium saucepan set over medium-high heat. When the sugar begins to melt, add enough water to cover, about 2/3 cup (160 ml). Boil 1 minute, add the remaining 1/2 cup (100 g) sugar, and boil 5 minutes, or until the sugar has dissolved and the mixture has thickened. Transfer to the prepared baking sheet and allow to cool.

BANANA TARTE TATIN

1¹/₂ cups (215 g) all-purpose (plain) flour
1 tablespoon granulated sugar
¹/₂ teaspoon salt
1¹/₂ cups (3 sticks) (330 g) unsalted butter
1 large egg yolk
¹/₄ cup (60 ml) cold water
1 cup (155 g) packed light-brown sugar
6 medium firm ripe bananas
2 tablespoons dark rum

The traditional French tarte tatin is transformed into a tropical treat by substituting bananas for apples and adding a touch of rum to the caramel. Whole bananas are sautéed in a buttery caramel sauce, topped with a rich crust while still in the pan, and then transferred to a hot oven, where the crust bakes until golden. Then the tart is turned upside down, so the sweet, golden caramel drips over the baked bananas nestled in buttery pastry. Serve with whipped cream.

Yield: 1 9-inch (23-cm) tart

Put the flour, sugar, and salt in a food processor and pulse 3 times. Cut 1 stick (110 g) of the butter into 8 pieces and add it to the flour mixture. Pulse 3 times, then process until the mixture resembles bread crumbs. Add the egg yolk and pulse to combine. With the motor running, add the water, 2 spoonfuls at a time. This will take about 5 seconds. Be careful not to overprocess; the dough should just be coming together. Place the dough on a floured surface and form into a ball, then flatten into a disc. Cover with plastic wrap (cling film) and refrigerate 30 minutes.

Preheat the oven to 400°F (200°C). Heat the remaining 2 sticks (220 g) butter in a heavy 9-inch (23-cm) skillet with an ovenproof handle set over medium heat. Stir in the brown sugar and cook 5 minutes. Meanwhile, peel the bananas. Arrange the bananas attractively in the pan, fitting them as close together as you can without squashing. Sprinkle with the rum and cook 10 minutes, or until the sauce begins to caramelize and the bananas start to brown on the bottom.

PACIFIC PALATE

BANANA TARTE TATIN (continued)

While the bananas are cooking, roll the dough out on a floured surface into a 10-inch (25-cm) circle. Lay the dough over the bananas, pressing the edges inside the rim of the pan. Work fast so the dough does not soften from the heat.

Transfer the pan to the oven and bake about 20 minutes, or until deep golden brown. Remove from the oven and let rest 5 minutes. Run a knife gently around the edge of the pan to loosen the pie from the sides. Place a serving dish upside down on top of the pan. Holding the dish firmly against the pan, grasp the handle (with an oven mitt, as it will be quite hot) and quickly turn the pan upside down. Lift the pan gently and loosen any bananas still sticking to the pan with a knife. Smooth any caramel remaining in the pan over the bananas. Serve warm or at room temperature with whipped cream.

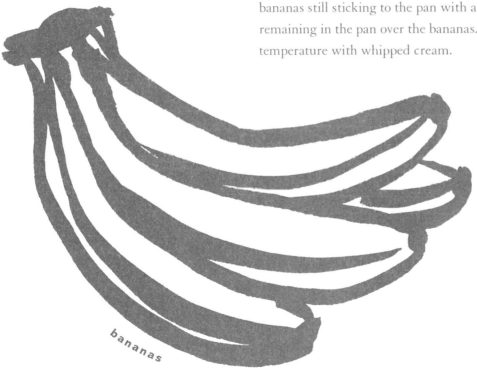

bananas

STAR FRUIT AND CHOCOLATE DESSERT

Vegetable oil for greasing pan
1 pound (450 g) bittersweet chocolate
2 cups (500 ml) heavy (double) cream
4 small star fruit (carambolas) without
    blemishes (about 1 1/2 pounds/675 g)
Mint sprigs for garnish
Mint Sauce (page 215)

Serve this spectacular dessert with champagne for a special occasion. It is easy to make and can be prepared well in advance. If star fruit are not available, substitute peeled kiwi fruit.

Yield: 1 loaf

Oil an 8 1/2 × 4 1/2 × 2 1/2-inch (21.6 cm × 11.4 cm × 6.4-cm) loaf pan. Cut a piece of parchment paper 4 1/2 inches (11.4 cm) wide and 16 inches (40.6 cm) long, and line the bottom of the pan with it, allowing the excess to hang over the edges of the pan (this will aid in removing the loaf from the pan).

Break the chocolate into 1-inch (2.5-cm) chunks. Put it in a food processor, pulse 5 times, then process to finely chop, about 1 minute. Put the cream in a small saucepan set over low heat and bring to a simmer. With the motor running, pour the hot cream through the feed tube and process until the chocolate is completely melted, about 15 seconds, stopping to scrape down the sides of the bowl as necessary. Pour one-third of the mixture into the prepared pan and refrigerate, allowing the remaining mixture to stand at room temperature.

Rinse the star fruit, pat dry, and trim 1/2 inch (1.3 cm) off each end. When the refrigerated chocolate mixture has partly set (about 20 minutes), arrange the fruit, end to end, on top of it down the center of the pan. Pour the remaining chocolate mixture over the fruit, smooth the top with a spatula, cover with plastic wrap (cling film), and refrigerate overnight.

To serve, run a knife around the edges of the pan to loosen the loaf. Lift the ends of the parchment and transfer the loaf to a chilled platter. Cut the loaf into 12 slices with a serrated knife. Place each slice in the center of a plate and surround it with Mint Sauce. Garnish with mint sprigs and serve immediately.

MINT SAUCE

30 mint leaves, finely chopped
2 cups (500 ml) milk
1/2 cup (100 g) sugar
4 large egg yolks

Yield: 2 3/4 cups

Put the mint and milk in a medium saucepan set over medium heat and bring to a boil. Remove from the heat and let sit 5 minutes. Strain, discarding the mint.

Put the sugar and egg yolks in a food processor and process 20 seconds. With the motor running, pour half the milk through the feed tube. Return the mixture to the saucepan and stir to mix with the remaining milk. Cook over low heat, stirring constantly, until the mixture coats a spoon, about 15 minutes.

Place the pan in a large bowl of ice and stir to cool the sauce. When cool, press plastic wrap (cling film) against the surface of the sauce, and refrigerate until ready to use.

star fruit

MACADAMIA·LIME MILE·HIGH MERINGUE TART

THE TART SHELL

*1/3 cup (45 g) finely ground macadamia
   nuts*

*1 1/4 cups (175 g) all-purpose (plain)
   flour plus more for rolling out
   the dough*

*12 tablespoons (1 1/2 sticks) (170 g)
   unsalted butter, chilled and cut into
   12 pieces*

2 tablespoons sugar

Pinch salt

1 large egg, lightly beaten

THE MERINGUE

3/4 cup (150 g) sugar

1/4 cup (60 ml) water

6 large egg whites

1/8 teaspoon cream of tartar

2 teaspoons coconut extract

THE FILLING

1/2 cup (100 g) sugar

Zest of 2 large limes

2 large eggs

*6 tablespoons (90 g) unsalted butter,
   melted*

*1/2 cup (55 g) finely ground macadamia
   nuts*

3 tablespoons freshly squeezed lime juice

The addition of ground macadamia nuts gives the buttery crust and smooth filling quite a different flavor and consistency from traditional lime meringue pie.

Yield: 9-inch (23-cm) tart

To make the tart shell, put the 1/3 cup (45 g) nuts, flour, the 12 tablespoons (170 g) butter, the 2 tablespoons sugar, and salt in a food processor and pulse 10 times, or until the mixture resembles coarse meal. With the motor running, pour the egg through the feed tube and process until the dough holds together. Transfer the dough to a floured surface and press it into a disc. Cover tightly with plastic wrap (cling film) and place in the freezer for 20 minutes, then refrigerate at least 15 minutes more.

Preheat the oven to 400°F (200°C). Roll the dough out on a floured surface into an 11-inch (28-cm) circle. Carefully transfer to a 9-inch (23-cm) tart pan with a removable bottom and press into place. Prick the bottom and sides with a fork and refrigerate 30 minutes.

Put the pan on a baking sheet, line the shell with aluminum foil, and fill with dried beans or pie weights. Bake 15 minutes, remove the foil and beans or weights, and bake 5 minutes more, or until the pastry is set but not browned. Cool on a wire rack.

To make the meringue, put the 3/4 cup (150 g) sugar and the water in a small sauté pan set over medium-high heat and bring to a boil, stirring gently. Cover, reduce the heat to medium, and cook until the sugar dissolves, about 5 minutes. Remove the cover and cook 5 minutes more.

MACADAMIA-LIME MILE-HIGH MERINGUE TART (continued)

While the sugar is cooking, beat the egg whites with the cream of tartar in an electric mixer. Add the 2 teaspoons coconut extract and continue beating until soft peaks form. With the mixer running, slowly pour the hot syrup into the egg whites in a steady stream. Continue beating until the whites are shiny, stiff, and hold a peak, about 3 minutes.

To make the filling, put the $1/2$ cup (100 g) sugar and the zest in a food processor, pulse 3 or 4 times, then process until the zest is finely chopped, about 3 minutes. Add the eggs, melted butter, the $1/2$ cup (55 g) macadamia nuts, and the lime juice, and pulse 3 or 4 times, then process 10 seconds, or until well mixed.

Pour the filling into the shell and bake on a baking sheet 20 minutes. Top with the meringue, return to the oven, and bake about 8 minutes more, or until the meringue is deep golden. Remove to a wire rack and allow to cool completely. Remove the tart from the pan and cut with a sharp knife dipped in water for each slice.

TAPIOCA WITH TROPICAL FRUIT

2 ripe bananas, cut into ¹/₄-inch
    (6-mm) slices
1 ripe papaya (pawpaw), cut into
    ¹/₄-inch (6-mm) dice
3 tablespoons quick-cooking tapioca
2 cups (500 ml) coconut milk
1 cup (250 ml) water
¹/₃ cup (70 g) sugar
1 teaspoon vanilla extract
¹/₂ cup (45 g) grated coconut

Tapioca is a sweet, glutinous, chewy root, high in iron and calcium, enjoyed by more than half the world's people and seemingly abhorred by everyone else. Served steamed, baked, boiled like potatoes, or dried and pounded into meal for fritters, dumplings, and breads, tapioca is a staple throughout the Pacific. Cooked with coconut milk and topped with fresh fruit and grated coconut, tapioca makes a smooth, creamy dessert.

Yield: 6 servings

Divide the banana and papaya equally among 6 dessert bowls. Put the tapioca, coconut milk, water, and sugar in a 2-quart (2-l) microwave-safe baking dish, and let sit 5 minutes. Cover and microwave at full power 5 minutes, stopping occasionally to stir. Stir in the vanilla, then spoon the hot pudding over the fruit. Let cool to room temperature, then refrigerate. Sprinkle with grated coconut and serve chilled.

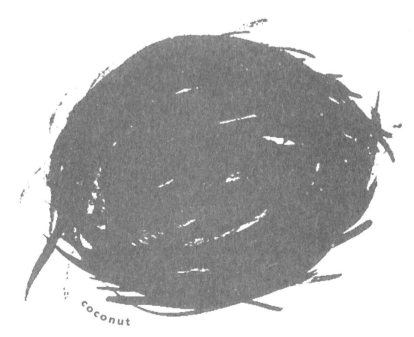

coconut

SWEET-AND-HOT TROPICAL FRUIT SALAD

2 tablespoons tamarind paste

2 tablespoons hot water

2 tablespoons packed brown sugar

1 small chili pepper, halved and seeded

3 tablespoons roasted unsalted peanuts
(groundnuts)

1 teaspoon salt

$^1/_2$ cucumber, halved lengthwise and
sliced thin

1 mango, cut into 1-inch (2.5-cm) cubes

$^1/_4$ pineapple, cut into 1-inch (2.5-cm)
cubes

1 jícama (about 6 ounces/170 g), peeled
and cut into 1-inch (2.5-cm) cubes

1 Asian pear, peeled and cut into 1-inch
(2.5-cm) cubes

This zesty dressing gives an unusual kick to the fresh fruit.

Yield: 6 servings

Soak the tamarind in the hot water 30 minutes. Strain, discarding the pulp. Put the tamarind liquid into a food processor along with the sugar, chili, peanuts, and salt. Process 30 seconds, stopping to scrape down the sides of the bowl as necessary.

In a large bowl toss together the cucumber, mango, pineapple, jícama, and Asian pear. Add the dressing and mix well just before serving.

HAUPIA WITH STAR FRUIT AND BANANA

13-ounce (370-ml) can coconut milk

1/4 cup (50 g) sugar

5 tablespoons (40 g) cornstarch
(cornflour)

3/4 cup (180 ml) water

1/2 cup (45 g) grated coconut

1/4 cup (60 ml) dark rum

2 medium star fruit (carambolas),
cut into 1/4-inch (6-mm) slices

3 apple bananas or other flavorful
banana, cut into 1/4-inch
(6-mm) slices

Sweet, smooth haupia is served throughout Polynesia, and no Hawaiian luau would be complete without it.

Yield: 8 servings

Put the coconut milk and sugar in a medium saucepan set over medium heat and bring to a boil. Add the cornstarch to the water and stir until smooth. Add the cornstarch slurry to the hot coconut milk and stir to blend. Pour the mixture into an 8 × 8-inch (20 × 20-cm) baking pan. Let cool to room temperature, then refrigerate to chill.

Cut into 2-inch (5-cm) squares. Heat a large, heavy skillet and toss in the coconut. Cook, stirring, until the coconut is browned. Add the rum and stir until it evaporates. Transfer the coconut to a flat dish and roll the haupia squares in it until they are well coated. Place 2 haupia squares on each plate and garnish with the star fruit and banana.

apple bananas

TROPICAL FRUIT GALETTE WITH MACADAMIA-NUT PASTE

Just about any tropical fruit can be baked in this thin, open-face crust layered with macadamia-nut paste to create a charming dessert.

Yield: 6 servings

THE GALETTE

1¹/₂ cups (215 g) all-purpose (plain) flour

12 tablespoons (1¹/₂ sticks) (170 g) unsalted butter, cut into ¹/₂-inch (1.3-cm) cubes

¹/₄ teaspoon salt

¹/₃ cup (80 ml) ice water

THE FILLING

¹/₃ cup (45 g) macadamia nuts

¹/₃ cup (70 g) packed raw brown sugar or light brown sugar

4 tablespoons (¹/₂ stick) (55 g) unsalted butter, cut into 4 pieces

1 large egg white

¹/₄ teaspoon vanilla extract

3 pounds (1.4 kg) ripe but firm tropical fruit, such as mango, banana, guava, or papaya, cut into ¹/₂-inch (1.3-cm) slices

Grated zest of 2 limes

¹/₃ cup (70 g) plus 1 teaspoon Demerara or turbinado or light brown sugar

¹/₂ cup (115 g) tropical fruit jelly, such as guava or Cape gooseberry

Two hours before you are ready to begin making the dough, put the flour and the 12 tablespoons (170 g) butter in the freezer.

Put the flour, butter, and salt in a food processor and process 5 seconds. Add the water and process 5 seconds more, or until the dough comes together. There will still be lumps of butter visible in the dough.

On a lightly floured surface, roll the dough out into a 15-inch (38-cm) circle. Transfer to a buttered baking sheet or pizza pan and chill in the freezer until firm, about 20 minutes, then refrigerate at least 20 minutes.

Preheat the oven to 400°F (200°C).

Put the nuts and brown sugar in a food processor, pulse 5 times, then process 30 seconds. Add the 4 tablespoons (55 g) butter and pulse 5 times. Add the egg white and vanilla, and process 15 seconds.

Spread the mixture evenly over the dough to within 2 inches (5 cm) of the edge. Arrange the fruit on top. Mix the zest with the sugar and sprinkle the mixture over the fruit. Fold the edges of the dough up over the fruit to create a 2-inch (5-cm) border. (If the dough is very firm and cold, wait a few minutes for it to soften to prevent it from cracking.) Sprinkle the border with the 1 teaspoon sugar.

Bake the galette about 45 minutes, or until the fruit is soft and the crust is golden brown. Spoon the jelly over the fruit and spread it evenly with a pastry brush. Let the galette cool to room temperature before serving.

BAKED VOLCANOES

(continued on next page)

THE CHOCOLATE WAFERS

4 ounces (115 g) semisweet (dark)
* chocolate*
3 tablespoons boiling water
1¼ cups (175 g) all-purpose (plain) flour
8 tablespoons (1 stick) (115 g) unsalted
* butter*
Pinch of salt

THE MERINGUE

1½ cups (300 g) sugar
½ cup (120 ml) water
8 large egg whites
¼ teaspoon almond extract

Fresh pineapple topped with chocolate wafers and mango sorbet are wrapped in a swirl of bronzed and bright-red meringue to resemble a volcanic eruption with flowing lava. This dramatic presentation can be assembled up to a day in advance.

Yield: 4 servings

MAKE THE WAFERS. Break the chocolate into pieces and put it in a food processor. Pulse 6 times, then process 15 seconds to coarsely chop. With the motor running, pour the boiling water through the feed tube. Continue to process until the chocolate is completely melted. Transfer to a bowl and allow to cool.

Put the flour, butter, and salt in the food processor and process 10 seconds, or until the mixture resembles coarse meal. Add the melted chocolate and pulse 10 times, or until thoroughly combined, then process until the dough forms a ball.

Roll the dough into a cylinder and cut into 8 pieces. Flatten each piece into a disc and wrap in plastic wrap (cling film). Place the discs on a baking sheet and place in the freezer 30 minutes.

Preheat the oven to 375°F (190°C). Roll each disc out between 2 sheets of wax paper into a 4½-inch (11.4-cm) circle. Place the circles in their wax paper on the baking sheet and refrigerate 30 minutes. Peel off the top layer of wax paper. Put the baking sheet in the oven and bake the wafers 15 minutes, or until firm. Invert the wafers on their wax-paper backing onto a flat surface, and peel off the paper. Allow the wafers to cool completely.

MAKE THE MERINGUE. Put the sugar and water in a small saucepan set over medium-high heat and bring to a boil, stirring gently. Cover and cook until the sugar dissolves, about 5 minutes. Remove the cover and cook 5 minutes more.

BAKED VOLCANOES *(continued)*

(continued from previous page)

THE CHOCOLATE SPONGE

4 ounces (115 g) semisweet (dark)
   chocolate
2 tablespoons all-purpose (plain) flour
2 tablespoons cornstarch (cornflour)
4 large eggs, separated
1/2 teaspoon almond extract
Pinch salt
1/4 cup (50 g) sugar

THE ASSEMBLY

1 large ripe pineapple
1 1/2 teaspoons red food coloring
4 ounces (115 g) semisweet (dark)
   chocolate, melted
2 cups (450 g) mango sorbet

Beat the egg whites and almond extract in an electric mixer
until foamy. With the motor running, slowly pour the hot sugar
syrup into the egg whites in a steady stream. Continue beating
until the whites are shiny and form stiff peaks, about 3 minutes.

MAKE THE CHOCOLATE SPONGE. Preheat the oven to 400°F
(200°C). Butter a 15 1/2 × 10 1/2 × 1-inch (39 × 27 × 2.5-cm) jelly-
roll pan, line with parchment paper, and lightly butter and flour
the paper.

Break the chocolate into pieces and put it in the food processor.
Pulse 6 times, then process 15 seconds to coarsely chop. Mix the
flour with the cornstarch, and sift the mixture on top of the
chocolate. Pulse 6 times, then process 5 seconds.

In a medium bowl beat together the egg yolks and almond
extract.

Beat the egg whites in an electric mixer until foamy. Add
the salt, then, with the motor running, gradually add the sugar,
continuing to beat until the whites form stiff peaks. Fold one-third
of the whites into the yolk mixture, then pour this mixture over
the remaining whites. Add the chocolate-flour mixture and fold
gently to combine.

Spread the batter evenly in the prepared pan and bake 10 minutes, or until the cake springs back when touched. When the cake
has cooled, cut out 4 4 1/2-inch (11.4-cm) circles.

ASSEMBLE THE VOLCANOES. Trim the ends off the pineapple. Cut
the unpeeled pineapple into 4 slices about 1 1/2 inches (4 cm) thick.
Cut a ring around the core of each slice, and cut the flesh into
4 sections. With the tip of the knife, cut a ring about 3/4 inch (2 cm)
inside the peel and 1 inch (2.5 cm) deep; be careful not to cut

through to the bottom. Using a melon baller, scoop out the pineapple flesh inside the ring and around the core, and reserve. Cut out the core and discard to form bowl-shaped pieces of pineapple.

Put the reserved pineapple flesh in the food processor, pulse 5 times, then process 5 seconds to purée. Transfer to a large bowl and fold in 1 cup of the meringue. Add the food coloring to the remaining meringue and fold to distribute the color evenly. Add more color if necessary; it should be deep red.

Cut out 4 parchment squares a little larger than the pineapple slices, and place them on a foil-lined baking sheet. Place the pineapple bowls on the parchment squares. Fill each bowl with the pineapple-meringue mixture. Top with a chocolate wafer, then a sponge circle. Spread with melted chocolate and top with another wafer. Top this with sorbet, smoothing it into a mound. Working quickly, cover the sorbet completely with meringue, smoothing it upward with a spatula to form a volcano-shaped peak. Spoon the red meringue on top, allowing some to run down the sides in rivulets to resemble flowing lava. (The baking sheet can be placed in the freezer at this point until you are ready to serve.)

Preheat the oven to 400°F (200°C). Place the baking sheet on the lowest rack of the oven and bake until the meringue has browned all over, about 7 minutes. Lifting them by their parchment paper, transfer the volcanoes to individual dessert plates. Carefully slide the paper out from under the volcanoes and serve immediately.

baked volcano

COCONUT-RUM CHEESECAKE

THE CRUST

10 whole graham crackers
3 tablespoons packed light-brown sugar
3 tablespoons dark rum

THE FILLING

*1½ pounds (675 g) fat-free cream
    cheese, chilled*
1 cup (155 g) packed light-brown sugar
Egg substitute equivalent to 3 large eggs
1 tablespoon imitation coconut extract

THE TOPPING

1 cup (250 ml) fat-free sour cream
2 tablespoons granulated sugar
2 tablespoons dark rum
*Sliced tropical fruit, such as mango,
    pineapple, star fruit (carambolas),
    and kiwi*
3 tablespoons apricot jam
1 tablespoon water

Virtually no fat, no cholesterol, yet still rich and creamy like traditional cheesecake.

Yield: 1 9-inch (23-cm) cake

Preheat the oven to 350°F (175°C). Put the graham crackers and 3 tablespoons brown sugar in a food processor and process to finely grind. Add the 3 tablespoons rum and pulse until the crumbs are just moistened. Using a paper towel (kitchen paper) or a spoon moistened with water, press the crumb mixture onto the bottom of a 9-inch (23-cm) springform pan with 3-inch (7.5 cm) sides. Bake until the crust is dry and slightly puffed, about 10 minutes. (Do not turn off the oven.) Cool on a rack.

To make the filling, process the cream cheese and 1 cup (155 g) brown sugar until smooth. Add the egg substitute and extract, and process to blend. Pour the filling into the crust and bake until the filling begins to crack around the edges and the center moves only slightly when shaken, about 40 minutes. (Do not turn off the oven.)

To make the topping, mix the sour cream, granulated sugar, and 2 tablespoons rum in a small bowl. Spread evenly over the hot cheesecake and bake 10 minutes. Allow to cool completely, then cover with foil and refrigerate overnight.

To serve, run a knife around the sides of the pan to loosen the cake, and remove the springform. Overlap fruit slices decoratively on top of the cake. Put the jam and water in a small saucepan set over medium heat and cook until the jam melts. Strain and brush the glaze over the fruit.

INGREDIENTS AND SUBSTITUTIONS

Ahi Hawaiian name for bigeye and yellowfin tuna. Ahi can reach up to 250 pounds (114 kg). The deep red flesh has a high fat content. Best cooked quickly and served rare (it is often used as sashimi) or blackened with the center left rare. Substitute any fresh tuna.

Aku Skipjack tuna, with a firmer, darker flesh than ahi. Often used in poke (raw marinated fish). Substitute any fresh tuna.

aku

Banana A staple of the Polynesian people. About twenty different varieties are grown on all the islands, from small, delicate apple bananas to plantains, which are eaten sautéed, baked, or sliced thin and fried like potato chips.

Bitter melon A spiny gourd used in Chinese and Filipino cooking.

Bok choy Asian cabbage. Substitute napa cabbage.

Breadfruit Also known as Ulu. A food staple throughout the Pacific. The fruit has a tough, bright-green skin mottled with occasional brown spots. When ripe, the flesh has a texture rather like a damp sponge and is creamy yellow in color. The flavor, apart from a light hint of banana, is on the bland side and because of this the fruit serves well as a starch in place of potatoes, rice, or bread. For many Pacific Islanders breadfruit is as much a staple as taro and banana. It can be cooked in the same way as any starchy root vegetable: baked and mashed with plenty of butter, boiled, or steamed for a few minutes, then cut in thin slices and fried like potato chips. As a substitute, use sweet potatoes.

breadfruit

daikon

Cellophane noodles Also called bean thread, long rice, or Oriental vermicelli, these clear noodles are made from a paste of mung-bean flour and water. They turn translucent and slippery when cooked.

Chili sauce Hot, spicy condiment made with chilies, garlic salt, and oil. Used in Chinese and Southeast Asian cooking. Substitute any hot sauce.

Chili water Mildly hot all-purpose condiment found in most Hawaiian restaurants along with shoyu.

Chinese five-spice powder A highly aromatic Chinese spice blend of star anise, cinnamon, clove, fennel seed, and Sichuan peppercorn.

Cilantro A distinctive, strong-flavored green herb also known as coriander or Chinese parsley. It is a member of the parsley family and native to the Middle East.

Coconut milk Coconuts were first introduced to Hawaii by migrating Polynesians, then later by Westerners, who brought with them about six more varieties. A coconut is mature when its husk turns brown. The nut is then pierced through its "eyes," three dark spots at one end, and the coconut water drained out. The nut is then cracked open. In an immature nut the meat is soft and jellylike and can be spooned out and eaten. It is often fed this way to babies. The mature meat is grated, soaked in water, and then squeezed. The resultant liquid is coconut milk and is different from the coconut water found inside the nut. Coconut milk can be bought canned or frozen. Be sure the milk you buy is unsweetened.

Daikon Long, creamy-white turnip common in Japanese and Korean dishes. Similar in flavor to radish, with a mild taste and crisp texture. Substitute radish.

Ginger Native to Asia, gingerroot (it is actually a rhizome) flourishes throughout the tropics and plays a prominent role in many Pacific and Asian cuisines. At its best when young, ginger is plump, juicy, and highly aromatic. Avoid using older ginger, which is drier and hotter. As ginger dehydrates easily, it is best stored in plastic bags in the refrigerator. For indefinite storage, place peeled pieces in airtight containers and cover with vodka (the vodka will not impair the flavor of the ginger). Rich in minerals and in vitamins A and B, ginger is also used to ease indigestion and for travel and sea sickness.

ginger

Guava This tart fruit with its yellow skin, pink flesh, and distinctive aroma can be eaten raw or cooked to make sauces and jellies. Several varieties grow wild on all the islands; in fact, they are considered a pest. The Big Island and Kauai grow guavas commercially for juice, canning, and purées. Chilled guava juice is commonly served at breakfast instead of orange juice.

Hawaiian salt Coarse sea salt similar to kosher salt. It has a natural red color that is the result of a high iron content. Substitute kosher salt.

Hoisin sauce Thick, sweet, garlicky sauce made from fermented soybeans common in Chinese and Southeast Asian cooking. It is customarily spread on thin pancakes and served with duck or used as a seasoning or condiment.

Jícama South American brown-skinned tuber with the texture of water chestnut and a delicate flavor. Used raw in salads or cooked. It ranges from the size of an apple to that of a cantaloupe.

Kaffir lime leaves These distinctive aromatic leaves are used in Southeast Asian cooking to flavor curries, soups, and sauces. Fresh leaves have a more intense flavor than dried. Substitute lime zest.

Kajiki Hawaiian name for Pacific blue marlin, also called a'u. The meat is very lean and can be broiled, poached, or stir-fried. Substitute swordfish or halibut.

jicama

kajiki

Lemon grass Grown throughout the tropics, this fragrant grass gives Thai cuisine its distinctive, light lemony-lime flavor. Use the creamy part of the stalk near the base to finely dice, or cut stalk into 3-inch (7.6-cm) pieces and add to dish. Remove before serving.

Lilikoi Passion fruit. This humble-looking fruit grows wild on vines throughout the tropics. It can be wrinkled with purplish-brown skin or smooth and plump with yellow-green skin. Tear open the skin, and an intense, exquisite aroma will pervade the air. The bright-orange pulp with its many dark little edible seeds can be eaten right out of the skin with a spoon, or scooped out and put through a strainer, the seeds discarded and the sieved liquid used in place of lemon or orange juice. Passion fruit juice can also be bought frozen, concentrated, or canned.

Limu Edible seaweed, usually used in poke (raw marinated fish), comes in about twenty-five varieties today, though it is believed that about forty varieties were once eaten by the Hawaiians. Commonly used as a condiment. The most popular are limu kohu, which is fine and has a reddish color, and limu lipoa, which is flat, light-brown, and has a perfumelike aroma of sea salt and is used much like pepper. In Japanese-influenced dishes it is common to use many types of seaweed, two of the most common being crunchy ogo and nori, the flat dried seaweed sheets used for wrapping sushi rolls.

Lotus root The root of the water lily. Lotus root is peeled and sliced into circles. It is often stir-fried with other vegetables. Its attractive creamy-white slices are slightly crunchy with a hint of sweetness.

sliced lotus root

lotus root

Macadamia nuts Native to Australia, these nuts were introduced to Hawaii about a hundred years ago and are grown commercially on the Big Island. This rich, creamy-colored nut is eaten as a snack and also used in cooking. It can be finely ground to thicken soups and sauces, chopped and sprinkled on salads, and, most popularly, used to enrich desserts. They are also eaten salted like peanuts. The oil is highly prized and used in dressings and cooking as a pleasant alternative to vegetable oil.

Mahimahi This light, firm, tender, pink-fleshed fish is also known as dolphin fish but is no relation to the mammal. The fish are caught in the open ocean and range in size from about 10 to 25 pounds (5 to 11 kg). Unfortunately, mahimahi has gotten a bad rap, as it most often appears on the typical tourist menu in a breaded, soggy, defrosted form that is usually over-cooked and rubbery. It is, however, an excellent and delicious fish when served fresh and not overcooked.

mahimahi

Mango Native to the Himalayas, mangoes are considerably better known than apples in more than half the world, where they are a staple, second only to bananas and coconuts. This fragrant fruit has been cultivated as long as 6,000 years, according to some estimates. There are many varieties, which range from slightly oval or kidney-shaped to almost round. The skin can be green to yellow-orange to yellow and crimson-colored. The most popular in the islands is the Hayden mango, which has a kidney shape and a pretty crimson blush when ripe. The Hayden is not quite as fibrous as many other varieties, and the flesh has a firm texture with a rich, fragrant mango flavor and a beautiful light pumpkin color. Ripe mangoes are eaten raw as a fruit, puréed, used in sauces and marinades, and diced and combined with other ingredients for salsas. Green mangoes are sliced thin and simmered to make chutney or pickles.

Maui onion Mild, white, sweet, and moist onion grown high on the slopes of Haleakala Volcano, where the rich volcanic soil, mild temperature, and rainfall create ideal growing conditions. Vidalia and Walla Walla onions are good substitutes.

Mirin Sweet rice wine used in Japanese and Chinese cooking to flavor marinades, glazes, and sauces. Substitute medium-dry sherry.

Miso Fermented thick soybean paste used in soups and stews. Miso ranges in color and texture from sweet and light to strong, dense, and dark.

Nori Thin sheets of dried seaweed used for wrapping sushi.

Onaga A bottom fish also called red snapper. Its moist, delicate pink flesh turns white when cooked. Can be steamed, baked, grilled, or sautéed. Monkfish and orange roughy are good substitutes.

Ono Also known as wahoo, it is a type of mackerel. Ono has white, flaky flesh and a firm texture that works well with marinades, whether steamed, sautéed, or grilled. Tuna and swordfish are good substitutes.

Opah Large, brightly colored bony fish also called moonfish. This open-ocean fish can range in weight from 60 to 200 pounds (27 to 91 kg) and has a fatty pinkish flesh that is well suited to sauces. Serve poached, steamed, or baked. Good substitutes are turbot, swordfish, and halibut.

Opakapaka Also called pink snapper. Highly delicate and moist with firm pink flesh that turns white when cooked. Can be cooked using all methods. Is often eaten raw as sashimi. Substitutes are any snapper, monkfish, and sea bass.

opah

Opal basil A very popular basil in Southeast Asian dishes. With its dark purple stems and deep emerald leaves lined with purple veins, opal basil has a noticeable anise flavor. Also popular in Thai food is lemon basil, which has small, narrow, light-green leaves. If these basils are hard to find, you can certainly use the more common type of basil.

Opihi Small black limpets with a taste similar to oysters usually used in poke (raw marinated fish). Dangerous to harvest, as they grow in rocky shoreline areas, opihi is expensive and highly prized.

Rice vinegar Vinegar with about half the acidity of cider vinegar.

Shiitake Broad group of highly fragrant black mushrooms used in Chinese and Japanese cooking, available dried or fresh. Dried shiitakes must be reconstituted in water before using.

Shoyu Japanese name for soy sauce. The variety used in Hawaii is a little sweeter and less salty than Chinese soy sauce.

Soba Japanese buckwheat noodles. Available fresh or dried.

Soy milk A nondairy liquid made by pressing cooked soybeans. Soy milk has one-third the fat and the same amount of protein as cow's milk, and contains no cholesterol. It also has fifteen times the iron of dairy milk.

Tahini A thick, buttery paste made from ground sesame seeds.

Tamari A byproduct of the miso-making process similar to shoyu or soy sauce, which it can be used in place of.

Tamarind paste A sour, tangy paste that is often used like lemon juice in Southeast Asian, Indian, Filipino, and Middle Eastern cooking, though its acidity is quite different from that of citrus fruit. Tamarind is an unlikely looking candidate for the food pot. The dingy brown pods are 4 to 6 inches (10 to 15 cm) in length and look like shriveled old beans. Inside are large seeds resembling dates surrounded by a sticky pulp. This homely pod is the fruit of the dramatic and beautiful Tamarind tree, which grows to great heights in tropical zones and can be found gracing many city parks. It is also a favorite haunt for noisy Indian mynah birds. Tamarind generally comes in dark-brown plastic-wrapped blocks. You break off as much as needed and soak it in a little tepid water. The liquid is then drained for use in the recipe, and the seeds and pulp discarded. Available in Asian and Hispanic grocery stores.

opal basil

Taro A highly nutritious starchy tuber that is a staple of Polynesian cooking. Taro is traditionally made into poi, diced and added to stews, mashed and used to thicken sauces, or sliced thin and deep-fried to make chips. The root is white with thin purple veins that when cooked blend to make the taro a purplish-gray. Taro is fairly bland and so mixes well with spicy foods. The leaves of the taro plant are called luau leaves and are eaten much the same way as spinach.

taro root

They are also used to wrap a number of traditional Polynesian dishes or added to seafood stews. A word of warning: taro contains calcium oxalate crystals, which irritate the skin, so it must not be eaten raw. It is advisable to wear rubber gloves when handling any part of the taro plant.

Ti leaf A member of the agave family, the ti plant has large shiny green leaves that are sometimes variegated with red. The leaves have a number of uses in Polynesian cooking. They are used to wrap food for steaming and baking. The leaf is often used to serve food on, or many leaves are laid out as a table cover before a meal. The leaf is also used to make skirts for dancers practicing the ancient style of hula called kahiko. For a substitute food wrapping use corn husks or parchment paper.

ti leaf

Tofu A high-protein food also known as soybean curd. Tofu has a light, creamy texture and a clean taste. It is available fresh in firm, extra-firm, or soft cakes. It is also available as silken tofu, which is produced within its package and will keep unopened for months. Use tofu in dishes that call for chicken or fish, like stir-fries, fillings, and soups.

Udon Thick Japanese wheat noodles.

Umeboshi Sour unripe plums fermented in salt and used as a seasoning agent. Also available as a vinegar.

Wasabi Also referred to as Japanese horseradish, this very hot green root of the wasabi plant is available as a paste or in powdered form, which is then mixed with water. Wasabi is commonly mixed with shoyu and served with sashimi.

Wonton wrappers Thin rice-paper or egg-noodle wrappers used to make dumplings. Usually about 3 inches (7.6 cm) square, and the thinner, the better. Can be purchased fresh or frozen.

SOURCES FOR INGREDIENTS

The recipes in this book use a number of Asian ingredients that may not be available at the supermarket. Check your local yellow pages for Asian and Hispanic markets and health food stores in the area. Health food stores in particular are a great resource, as many of the ingredients used in these recipes are commonly available in these stores. If any ingredients are not stocked, health food store staff are generally quite knowledgeable about exotic ingredients and may be able to direct you to a source or order for you through the store.

Books are another great source of information. The following are particularly helpful with regard to exotic ingredients and Oriental and Asian foods: *Far Eastern Cookery* by Madhur Jaffrey (Harper & Row, 1989); *Uncommon Fruits and Vegetables. A Common Sense Guide* by Elizabeth Schneider (Harper & Row, 1986); *Friendly Foods* by Brother Ron Pickarski (Ten Speed Press, 1991); and *Hawaiian and Pacific Foods: A Book of Culinary Customs and Recipes Adapted for the American Hostess* by Katherine Bazore (M. Barrows & Co. Inc., 1963).

INDEX

(Page numbers in *italics* refer to illustrations.)

Ahi, 226
    and Jalapeño Maki, 33
    Jícama, and Ginger Maki, 34
    Sesame-Ginger-Crusted, 131
    Shoyu Poke, 41
Aioli, Citrus, Grilled Salmon with, 133
Aku, 117, *118*, 226, *226*
Almond Paste, in Banana Spring Rolls, 206–7
Appetizers. *See* Pupus
Artichoke, Shiitake, and Gorgonzola Pizza, 105
Avocado(s):
    Fettuccine with Tomatillos and, Mexican,
        178
    Guacamole, 197
    Paradise Salad, Pacific, 83
    and Shrimp Maki, 35
    Soba and Vegetable Maki, 32

Balsamic Honey Dijon Dressing, 98
Bamboo Shoot Pickle, 195
Banana(s), 226
    Haupia with Star Fruit and, 220
    Lentil, and Rosemary Salad, 85
    Raisin Chutney, 192
    Spring Rolls, 206–7
    Tapioca with Tropical Fruit, 218
    Tarte Tatin, 212–13
    Tropical Fruit—Stuffed Vine Leaves, 38
Bars, Passion, 205
Basil:
    Lobster and Scallop Bisque with, 78–79
    opal, 231, *231*
    Opal-, Coconut Soup, 69
    Papaya Purée, 198
    Tomato Filo Pizza, 107
Bean(s):
    Vegetable Soup with Cilantro Pesto, 70–71
    see also Black bean
Bean sprouts:
    Sesame Soba Salad, 90

Udon with Vegetables and Gado-Gado
    Sauce, 176
Beef, in Coconut Meatballs, 43
Beverages, 12–21
    Frosty Floral Fruit Lei, 21
    Ginger Bia, Hawaiian, 20
    Ginger Limeade, 19
    Guava Colada, 16
    Mai Tai, 15
    Margarita, 15
    Margarita Elena, 16
    Passion Fruit Champagne Cocktail, 17
    Pineapple Punch, 19
    Plantation Tea, Pacific, 21
    Sangría, Pacific, 18
Bia, Hawaiian Ginger, 20
Bisques:
    Lobster and Scallop, with Basil, 78–79
    Sweet Potato and Pear, 73
Bitter melon, 226
Black bean:
    and Feta Quesadilla, 45
    Soup, Tropical, 68
Bok choy:
    Stir-Fry, 164
    Udon with Vegetables and Gado-Gado
        Sauce, 176
Bouillabaisse, Pacific, 77
Breadfruit, 8, 226, *226*
    Ulussoise, 72
Broccoli:
    Salad, Five-Spice, 88
    Sesame Soba Salad, 90
Brunch dishes, 48–63
    Baked Eggs with Spinach in Crumb Crust,
        56–57
    Citrus Muffins with Smoked Turkey and
        Guava Jelly, 52
    Coconut-Corn Fritters, 59
    Eggs Benedict, Pacific, 53
    Shrimp Fritters, 62
    Spiced Pumpkin Fritters, 58
    Sweet Potato Fritters with Goat Cheese, 61
    Torte, 54–55

Zucchini Fritters, 60
Bulgur, in Tabbouleh, 44
Butternut Squash, Curried Ragout of Chicken
    with, 154

Caesar Dressing, 95
Cakes, Tofu, 165
Calamari Rings, 42
Candied Orange Peel, 211
Cardamom, 137–38
Cashew-Coconut Chicken, Spicy, 142
Celeriac and Mushroom Galette, 110
Cellophane noodles, 226–27
Champagne:
    Passion Fruit Cocktail, 17
    Sangría, Pacific, 18
Cheese:
    Brunch Torte, 54–55
    Feta and Black Bean Quesadilla, 45
    Feta and Leafy Green Galette, 111
    Gorgonzola, Shiitake, and Artichoke Pizza,
        105
    Parmesan, in Caesar Dressing, 95
    Parmesan Filo Pizza with Spinach, 106
    see also Goat cheese
Cheesecake, Coconut-Rum, 225
Chicken, 136–55
    Curried Lemon-Lime, 151
    Curried Ragout of, with Butternut Squash,
        154
    Drumsticks, Spicy, 152
    Grilled Ginger, 155
    Lime-Cilantro, 150
    Paella Pacifica, 122–23
    Papaya Skewers, 139
    Salad Tartlets, Pacific, 46
    Satay, 149
    Satay Pizza, 103
    Spicy Coconut-Cashew, 142
    Stir-Fry, Spicy Lemon-Ginger, 141
    in Sun-Dried-Tomato Sauce, 145
    Tropical Spicy, 144
    Wings, Fiery Chili, 153
    Wings, Sesame, 148

Chickpea(s):
    Eggplant, and Tomato Salad, 89
    Hummus, 198
    Hummus, Vine Leaves Stuffed with Squash,
        Tabbouleh and, 44
Chili:
    Chicken Wings, Fiery, 153
    Cinnamon Sauce, Eggplant in, 166
    sauce, 227
    water, 227
Chilies, roasting, 187
Chinese, 6, 8–9, 201–2
Chinese New Year, 201–2
Chocolate:
    Baked Volcanoes, 222–24
    Coconut Florentines, 210
    Mousse, in Banana Spring Rolls, 206–7
    and Star Fruit Dessert, 214
Chutneys, 186–87
    Banana-Raisin, 192
    Mango, 194
    Pineapple, 193
Cilantro, 227
    Lime Chicken, 150
    Lime Hollandaise, 199
    Pesto, Vegetable Soup with, 70–71
    Sauce, Onaga with, 127
    Shrimp, and Jícama Maki, 31
Cinnamon:
    Chili Sauce, Eggplant in, 166
    Ginger Canoes with Piña Colada Granita,
        208
Citrus:
    Aioli, Grilled Salmon with, 133
    Dressing, 99
    Muffins with Smoked Turkey and Guava
        Jelly, 52
    Pepper Shrimp Sauce, Pasta Shells with, 179
Clams, in Seafood Curry, 125
Coconut, 7
    Cashew Chicken, Spicy, 142
    Corn Fritters, 59
    Florentines, 210
    Mango Salsa, 191
    Meatballs, 43
    milk, 7, 8, 39, 59, 69, 74, 82, 87, 125, 138,
        140, 142, 149, 151, 162, 177, 191, 198,
        203, 218, 220, 227
    Opakapaka, Spicy, 126
    Opal-Basil Soup, 69

Rum Cheesecake, 225
Sauce, Duck in, 140
Colada:
    Guava, 16
    Piña, Granita, 209
    Piña, Granita, Ginger-Cinnamon Canoes
        with, 208
Coriander, 138
Corn:
    Coconut Fritters, 59
    Cups or Tartlet Shells, 168
Couscous-nut stuffing, 146
Crab Empanadas, 27
Cucumber:
    Gazpacho, Tropical, 67
    Paradise Salad, Pacific, 83
    Soba and Vegetable Maki, 32
    Udon with Vegetables and Gado-Gado
        Sauce, 176
    Yogurt Sauce, 199
Curry(ied), 138
    Chicken, Lemon-Lime, 151
    Chicken, Spicy Coconut-Cashew, 142
    Chicken, Tropical Spicy, 144
    Chicken in Sun-Dried-Tomato Sauce, 145
    Chicken Ragout with Butternut Squash, 154
    Duck in Coconut Sauce, 140
    Seafood, 125

Daikon, 227, 227
Desserts, 200–225
    Baked Volcanoes, 222–24
    Banana Spring Rolls, 206–7
    Banana Tarte Tatin, 212–13
    Candied Orange Peel, 211
    Coconut Florentines, 210
    Coconut-Rum Cheesecake, 225
    Ginger-Cinnamon Canoes with Piña Colada
        Granita, 208
    Haupia with Star Fruit and Banana, 220
    Macadamia-Lime Mile-High Meringue
        Tart, 216–17
    Passion Bars, 205
    Piña Colada Granita, 209
    Star Fruit and Chocolate, 214
    Sweet-and-Hot Tropical Fruit Salad, 219
    Tapioca with Tropical Fruit, 218
    Tropical Fruit Galette with Macadamia-Nut
        Paste, 221
Dijon Balsamic Honey Dressing, 98

Dipping Sauce, Sushi, 29
Dressings. See Salad dressings
Duck:
    in Coconut Sauce, 140
    Roast, in Tangerine Sauce, 146–47
Dumplings (Fragrant Orange Pot Stickers), 36

Eggplant:
    Baked, with Sun-Dried-Tomato Sauce, 169
    in Cinnamon-Chili Sauce, 166
    Ratatouille, Oriental, 167
    Soba with Sautéed Vegetables, 174
    Tomato, and Chickpea Salad, 89
Eggs:
    Baked, with Spinach in Crumb Crust, 56–57
    Benedict, Pacific, 53
    Brunch Torte, 54–55
Empanadas, Crab, 27
Entrées:
    Ahi, Sesame-Ginger-Crusted, 131
    Chicken, Curried Lemon-Lime, 151
    Chicken, Curried Ragout of, with Butternut
        Squash, 154
    Chicken, Grilled Ginger, 155
    Chicken, Lime-Cilantro, 150
    Chicken, Spicy Coconut-Cashew, 142
    Chicken, Tropical Spicy, 144
    Chicken Drumsticks, Spicy, 152
    Chicken in Sun-Dried-Tomato Sauce, 145
    Chicken Papaya Skewers, 139
    Chicken Satay, 149
    Chicken Stir-Fry, Spicy Lemon-Ginger, 141
    Chicken Wings, Fiery Chili, 153
    Chicken Wings, Sesame, 148
    Duck, Roast, in Tangerine Sauce, 146–47
    Duck in Coconut Sauce, 140
    Mahimahi in Tangerine Sauce, 130
    Onaga with Cilantro Sauce, 127
    Ono with Macadamia Nuts and Lime, 129
    Opakapaka, Spicy Coconut, 126
    Paella Pacifica, 122–23
    Paradise Salad, Pacific, 83
    Pineapple, Jícama, and Tofu Salad, 84
    Salmon, Grilled, with Citrus Aioli, 133
    Salmon in Filo with Spinach-Lime Soufflé,
        120–21
    Scallop and Shrimp Stir-Fry, 124
    Seafood Curry, 125
    Seafood Salad, Marinated, 87
    Shrimp Sauté, Spicy, 134

Swordfish, Seared Marinated, 135
Swordfish Skewers, Spice Island, 128
see also Galettes; Pasta; Pizzas; Vegetable
  entrées
Evil Jungle Prince, 162

Feta:
  and Black Bean Quesadilla, 45
  and Leafy Green Galette, 111
Fettuccine:
  with Shiitake-Lobster Sauce, 180
  with Tomatillos and Avocado, Mexican, 178
Fiery Chili Chicken Wings, 153
Filipinos, 7, 10, 203
Filo:
  Banana Spring Rolls, 206–7
  Pizza, Parmesan, with Spinach, 106
  Pizza, Tomato-Basil, 107
  Salmon in, with Spinach-Lime Soufflé,
    120–21
First courses. *See* Pupus.
Fish and seafood, 112–35, *118*
  Ahi, Sesame-Ginger-Crusted,
    131
  Bouillabaisse, Pacific, 77
  Calamari Rings, 42
  Crab Empanadas, 27
  Grilled Fish in Hot Tamarind Sauce, 132
  Lobster and Scallop Bisque with Basil,
    78–79
  Lobster-Shiitake Sauce, Fettuccine with, 180
  Mahimahi in Tangerine Sauce,
    130
  Marinated Seafood Salad, 87
  Onaga with Cilantro Sauce, 127
  Ono with Macadamia Nuts and Lime, 129
  Opakapaka, Spicy Coconut, 126
  Paella Pacifica, 122–23
  Scallop and Shrimp Stir-Fry, 124
  Scallops in Lime Juice, 39
  Seafood Curry, 125
  Seafood Soup, Hawaiian, 74
  smoked, in Pacific Eggs Benedict, 53
  Swordfish, Seared Marinated,
    135
  Swordfish Skewers, Spice Island, 128
  see also Ahi; Salmon; Shrimp
Five-spice:
  Broccoli Salad, 88
  powder, Chinese, 138, 227

Floral Fruit Lei, Frosty, 21
Florentines, Coconut, 210
French-inspired dishes:
  Banana Tarte Tatin, 212–13
  Bouillabaisse, Pacific, 77
  Maui Onion Soup with Goat Cheese Toasts,
    76
  Ratatouille, Oriental, 167
  Vegetable Soup with Cilantro Pesto, 70–71
  see also Galettes
Fritters:
  Coconut-Corn, 59
  Pumpkin, Spiced, 58
  Shrimp, 62
  Sweet Potato, with Goat Cheese, 61
  Zucchini, 60
Frosty Floral Fruit Lei, 21
Fruit:
  Lei, Frosty Floral, 21
  see also specific fruits

Gado-Gado Sauce, 177
  Udon with Vegetables and, 176
Galettes, 102, 108–11
  Leafy Green and Feta, 111
  Mushroom and Celeriac, 110
  Pastry for, 108
  Sweet Potato, Hawaiian, 109
  Tropical Fruit, with Macadamia-Nut Paste,
    221
Garlic:
  roasting, 187
  Sauce, 63
Gazpacho, Tropical, 67
Ginger, 227, *227*
  Ahi, and Jícama Maki, 34
  Bia, Hawaiian, 20
  Chicken, Grilled, 155
  Cinnamon Canoes with Piña Colada
    Granita, 208
  -Crusted Ahi, 131
  Lemon Chicken Stir-Fry, Spicy, 141
  Limeade, 19
  Papaya-Seed Dressing, Creamy, 96
  Tomato Salsa, 191
Goat cheese:
  Sweet Potato Fritters with, 61
  Toasts, Maui Onion Soup with, 76
  Tomatoes Stuffed with, 43
  with Tricolored Pepper Pizza, 104

Gorgonzola, Shiitake, and Artichoke Pizza, 105
Granita, Piña Colada, 209
  Ginger-Cinnamon Canoes with, 208–9
Grilled:
  Chicken, Ginger, 155
  Chicken Drumsticks, Spicy, 152
  Fish in Hot Tamarind Sauce, 132
  Papaya Chicken Skewers, 139
  Salmon with Citrus Aioli, 133
Guacamole, 197
Guava, 227–28
  Colada, 16
  Jelly, Citrus Muffins with Smoked Turkey
    and, 52

Haupia with Star Fruit and Banana, 220
Hawaii:
  culinary influences in, 6–11
  pupu parties in, 23
Hawaiian dishes:
  Ahi Shoyu Poke, 41
  Cherry Tomatoes Stuffed with Salmon, 40
  Ginger Bia, 20
  Seafood Soup, 74
  Sweet Potato Galette, 109
Hawaiian salt, 228
Herb(s):
  Fresh-, Pasta, 182
  see also specific herbs
Hoisin sauce, 228
Hollandaise, Cilantro-Lime, 199
Hominy, in Posole, 159
Honey Balsamic Dijon Dressing, 98
Hong Kong dishes:
  Fragrant Orange Pot Stickers, 36
  Hot-and-Sour Shrimp, 75
Hot-and-Sour Shrimp Soup, 75
Hummus, 198
  Vine Leaves Stuffed with Squash, Tabbouleh
    and, 44

Imu, 7
Indonesian and Indonesian-inspired dishes:
  Chicken, Spicy Coconut-Cashew, 142
  Chicken, Tropical Spicy, 144
  Chicken in Sun-Dried-Tomato Sauce, 145
  Duck in Coconut Sauce, 140
  Udon with Vegetables and Gado-Gado
    Sauce, 176
Indonesians, feasts of, 203

Ingredients, 226–33
    sources for, 233

Jalapeño and Ahi Maki, 33
Japanese, 6, 9, 202
    see also Sushi
Jícama, 228, *228*
    Ahi, and Ginger Maki, 34
    and Onion Pickle, 196
    Pineapple, and Tofu Salad, 84
    Shrimp, and Cilantro Maki, 31

Kaffir lime leaves, 228
Kajiki, 116, *118, 228, 228*
Kimchee, 9
Koreans, 6, 9, 202

Leafy Green and Feta Galette, 111
Lei, Frosty Floral Fruit, 21
Lemon:
    Ginger Chicken Stir-Fry, Spicy, 141
    Lime Chicken, Curried, 151
    Tahini Dressing, 99
    Thyme Dressing, 95
Lemon grass, 10, 149, 162, *162,* 228
Lentil, Banana, and Rosemary Salad, 85
Lilikoi. *See* Passion fruit
Lime:
    Cilantro Chicken, 150
    Cilantro Hollandaise, 199
    Juice, Scallops in, 39
    Lemon Chicken, Curried, 151
    Macadamia Mile-High Meringue Tart,
        216–17
    Margarita, 15
    Ono with Macadamia Nuts and, 129
    Spinach Soufflé, Salmon in Filo with,
        120–21
Limeade, Ginger, 19
Limu, 229
Lobster:
    and Scallop Bisque with Basil, 78–79
    Shiitake Sauce, Fettuccine with, 180
Lotus root, 229, *229*
Luaus, 7
Lunch dishes:
    Orange-Macadamia Salad, 85
    Paradise Salad, Pacific, 83
    Pineapple Punch, 19
    Scallop and Shrimp Stir-Fry, 124

Seafood Salad, Marinated, 87
Shrimp Sauté, Spicy, 134
Spinach and Shiitake Mushroom Salad, 86
Macadamia nut(s), 229
    Lime Mile-High Meringue Tart, 216–17
    Ono with Lime and, 129
    Orange Salad, 85
    Passion Bars, 205
    Paste, Tropical Fruit Galette with, 221
    and Red Pepper Pesto, 197
Mahimahi, 115, 116–17, *118, 229, 229*
    in Tangerine Sauce, 130
Mai Tai, 15
Maki:
    Ahi, Jícama, and Ginger, 34
    Ahi and Jalapeño, 33
    Shrimp, Jícama, and Cilantro, 31
    Shrimp and Avocado, 35
    Soba and Vegetable, 32
Mango, 229–30
    Chutney, 194
    Coconut Salsa, 191
    Papaya-Mint Salsa, 188
    Pineapple Salsa, 188
    sorbet, in Baked Volcanoes, 222–24
    Sweet-and-Hot Tropical Fruit Salad, 219
Margarita, 15
    Elena, 16
Maui onion(s), 230
    Soup with Goat Cheese Toasts, 76
Meatballs, Coconut, 43
Meringue:
    Baked Volcanoes, 222–24
    Tart, Macadamia-Lime Mile-High, 216–17
Mexican and Mexican-inspired dishes:
    Black Bean and Feta Quesadilla, 45
    Black Bean Soup, Pacific, 68
    Coconut-Corn Fritters, 59
    Crab Empanadas, 27
    Fettuccine with Tomatillos and Avocado, 178
    Guacamole, 197
    Posole, 159
    Stuffed Poblano Peppers with Mole, 160
Middle Eastern-inspired dishes:
    Hummus, 198
    Tabbouleh, 44
    Vine Leaves Stuffed with Squash, Hummus,
        and Tabbouleh, 44
Mint:
    Papaya-Mango Salsa, 188

Sauce, 215
Mirin, 230
Miso, 230
    Dressing, Oil-Free, 97
Mole, 161
    Stuffed Poblano Peppers with, 160
Monchong, 117
Muffins, Citrus, with Smoked Turkey and
    Guava Jelly, 52
Mushroom(s):
    and Celeriac Galette, 110
    Sesame Soba Salad, 90
    Shiitake, and Spinach Salad, 86
    Wild, Udon Noodles with, 175
    see also Shiitake
Mussels, in Seafood Curry, 125

Noodles. *See* Pasta; Soba noodle(s); Udon
    noodles
Nori, 230
Nut(s):
    couscous stuffing, 146
    Paste, Spicy, 143
    see also Macadamia nut(s)

Onaga, 116, *118,* 230
    with Cilantro Sauce, 127
Onion(s):
    and Jícama Pickle, 196
    Maui, 230
    Maui, Soup with Goat Cheese Toasts, 76
Ono (wahoo), 116, *118,* 230
    with Macadamia Nuts and Lime, 129
Opah, 117, *118,* 230, *230*
Opakapaka, 116, *118,* 230
    Spicy Coconut, 126
Opal basil, 231, *231*
    Coconut Soup, 69
Opihi, 231
Orange(s):
    Coconut Florentines, 210
    Macadamia Salad, 85
    Peel, Candied, 211
    Pot Stickers, Fragrant, 36
    Sauce, Fragrant, 37
    Tropical-Fruit Salsa, 190

Paella Pacifica, 122–23
Pan-Fried Noodles, 183

Papaya:
   Basil Purée, 198
   Chicken Salad Tartlets, Pacific,
      46
   Chicken Skewers, 139
   Mango-Mint Salsa, 188
   Paradise Salad, Pacific, 83
   Pineapple Salsa, 192
   and Shrimp Skewers, 119
   Tapioca with Tropical Fruit, 218
   Tropical-Fruit Salsa, 190
Papaya-Seed Ginger Dressing, Creamy, 96
Paradise Salad, Pacific, 83
Parmesan:
   Caesar Dressing, 95
   Filo Pizza with Spinach, 106
Passion fruit (lilikoi), 204, 228
   Bars, 205
   Champagne Cocktail, 17
Pasta, 170–83
   cellophane noodles, 226–27
   Fettuccine with Shiitake-Lobster Sauce, 180
   Fettuccine with Tomatillos and Avocado,
      Mexican, 178
   Fresh-Herb, 182
   Pan-Fried Noodles, 183
   Shells with Citrus-Pepper Shrimp Sauce,
      179
   with Smoked Salmon and Watercress, 181
   see also Soba noodle(s); Udon noodles
Pastries:
   Chicken Salad Tartlets, Pacific,
      46
   Corn Cups or Tartlet Shells, 168
   Crab Empanadas, 27
Pear:
   Asian, in Sweet-and-Hot Tropical Fruit
      Salad, 219
   and Sweet Potato Bisque, 73
Pepper(s) (bell):
   Brunch Torte, 54–55
   Gazpacho, Tropical, 67
   Poblano, Stuffed, with Mole,
      160
   Ratatouille, Oriental, 167
   Red, and Macadamia Nut Pesto, 197
   Sesame Soba Salad, 90
   Tricolored, and Goat Cheese Pizza, 104
   Udon with Vegetables and Gado-Gado
      Sauce, 176

Pepper (red) and Citrus Shrimp Sauce, Pasta
   Shells with, 179
Pesto:
   Cilantro, Vegetable Soup with, 70–71
   Red Pepper and Macadamia Nut, 197
Pickles:
   Bamboo Shoot, 195
   Jícama and Onion, 196
Pie, Rosemary Scallop Potato, 163
Piña Colada Granita, 209
   Ginger-Cinnamon Canoes with, 208
Pineapple:
   Baked Volcanoes, 222–24
   Chutney, 193
   Jícama, and Tofu Salad, 84
   Mango Salsa, 188
   Papaya Salsa, 192
   Plantation Tea, Pacific, 21
   Punch, 19
   Sweet-and-Hot Tropical Fruit Salad, 219
   Tropical-Fruit Salsa, 190
   Tropical Fruit—Stuffed Vine Leaves, 38
Pizzas, 100–107
   Basic Dough for, 103
   Chicken Satay, 103
   Goat Cheese with Tricolored Pepper, 104
   Parmesan Filo, with Spinach,
      106
   Shiitake, Artichoke, and Gorgonzola, 105
   Tomato-Basil Filo, 107
Plantation Tea, Pacific, 21
Poblano Peppers, Stuffed, with Mole, 160
Poke, Ahi Shoyu, 41
Polynesians, 6, 7, 8, 200
Portuguese, 6, 9, 202–3
Posole, 159
Potato(es):
   Pie, Rosemary Scallop, 163
   see also Sweet potato
Pot Stickers, Fragrant Orange, 36
Pumpkin Fritters, Spiced, 58
Punches:
   Frosty Floral Fruit Lei for, 21
   Pineapple, 19
Pupus, 22–47
   Ahi Shoyu Poke, 41
   Black Bean and Feta Quesadilla, 45
   Calamari Rings, 42
   Cherry Tomatoes Stuffed with Salmon, 40
   Chicken Salad Tartlets, Pacific, 46

Coconut Meatballs, 43
Crab Empanadas, 27
Fragrant Orange Pot Stickers, 36
Scallops in Lime Juice, 39
serving, 25–26
Sushi Platter, Pacific, 28–35
Tomatoes Stuffed with Goat Cheese, 43
Tropical Fruit—Stuffed Vine Leaves, 38
Vine Leaves Stuffed with Squash, Hummus,
   and Tabbouleh, 44
see also Galettes; Pizzas

Quesadilla, Black Bean and Feta, 45

Ragout of Chicken with Butternut Squash,
   Curried, 154
Raisin(s):
   Banana Chutney, 192
   Tropical Fruit—Stuffed Vine Leaves, 38
Ratatouille, Oriental, 167
Rice, 9
   Paella Pacifica, 122–23
   Vinegar, 28
Rice vinegar, 231
Rosemary:
   Banana, and Lentil Salad, 85
   Scallop Potato Pie, 163
Rum:
   Coconut Cheesecake, 225
   Guava Colada, 16
   Mai Tai, 15

Salad(s), 80–91
   Banana, Lentil, and Rosemary, 85
   Broccoli, Five-Spice, 88
   Chicken, Tartlets, Pacific, 46
   Eggplant, Tomato, and Chickpea, 89
   Orange-Macadamia, 85
   Pacific Paradise, 83
   Pineapple, Jícama, and Tofu, 84
   Seafood, Marinated, 87
   Sesame Soba, 90
   Snowpea and Shiitake, 91
   Spinach and Shiitake Mushroom, 86
   Tabbouleh, 44
   Tropical Fruit, Sweet-and-Hot, 219
Salad dressings, 92–99
   Balsamic Honey Dijon, 98
   Caesar, 95
   Citrus, 99

Ginger Papaya-Seed, Creamy, 96
Lemon-Tahini, 99
Lemon-Thyme, 95
Miso, Oil-Free, 97
Sesame Soy, 97
Soyannaise, 98
Salmon:
Cherry Tomatoes Stuffed with, 40
in Filo with Spinach-Lime Soufflé, 120–21
Grilled, with Citrus Aioli, 133
Marinated Seafood Salad, 87
Smoked, Pasta with Watercress and, 181
Salsas, 184–86, 187
Coconut-Mango, 191
Mango-Pineapple, 188
Oriental, 189
Papaya-Mango-Mint, 188
Papaya-Pineapple, 192
Tomato-Ginger, 191
Tropical-Fruit, 190
Salt, Hawaiian, 228
Samoans, 6, 8
Sangría, Pacific, 18
Satay:
Chicken, 149
Chicken, Pizza, 103
Sauces:
Cilantro-Lime Hollandaise, 199
Gado-Gado, 177
Garlic, 63
Guacamole, 197
Hummus, 198
Mint, 215
Mole, 161
Orange, Fragrant, 37
Papaya-Basil Purée, 198
Red Pepper and Macadamia Nut Pesto, 197
Sushi Dipping, 29
Tangerine, 146–47
Yogurt-Cucumber, 199
see also Chutneys; Salsas
Scallop(s):
Bouillabaisse, Pacific, 77
in Lime Juice, 39
and Lobster Bisque with Basil, 78–79
Marinated Seafood Salad, 87
Seafood Curry, 125
Seafood Soup, Hawaiian, 74
and Shrimp Stir-Fry, 124
Scallop Potato Pie, Rosemary, 163

Seafood. See Ahi; Fish and seafood; Salmon;
    Shrimp
Seared Marinated Swordfish, 135
Sesame:
Chicken Wings, 148
Ginger-Crusted Ahi, 131
Soba Salad, 90
Soy Dressing, 97
Shiitake, 231
Artichoke, and Gorgonzola Pizza, 105
Lobster Sauce, Fettuccine with, 180
Mushroom and Celeriac Galette, 110
and Snowpea Salad, 91
and Spinach Salad, 86
Shoyu, 231
Shrimp:
and Avocado Maki, 35
Bouillabaisse, Pacific, 77
Citrus-Pepper, Sauce, Pasta Shells with, 179
Fritters, 62
Hot-and-Sour Soup, 75
Jícama, and Cilantro Maki, 31
Paella Pacifica, 122–23
and Papaya Skewers, 119
Sauté, Spicy, 134
and Scallop Stir-Fry, 124
Seafood Curry, 125
Seafood Soup, Hawaiian, 74
Skewers:
Chicken Satay, 149
Papaya Chicken, 139
Shrimp and Papaya, 119
Swordfish, Spice Island, 128
Snowpea and Shiitake Salad, 91
Soba noodle(s), 29, 231
cooking, 173
Salad, Sesame, 90
with Sautéed Vegetables, 174
and Vegetable Maki, 32
Soufflé, Spinach-Lime, Salmon in Filo with,
    120–21
Soups, 64–79
Black Bean, Tropical, 68
Bouillabaisse, Pacific, 77
Gazpacho, Tropical, 67
Hot-and-Sour Shrimp, 75
Lobster and Scallop Bisque with Basil,
    78–79
Maui Onion, with Goat Cheese Toasts, 76
Opal-Basil Coconut, 69

Seafood, Hawaiian, 74
Sweet Potato and Pear Bisque, 73
Ulussoise, 72
Vegetable, with Cilantro Pesto, 70–71
South Sea Islanders, 6
Soy:
milk, 231
Sesame Dressing, 97
Soyannaise, 98
Spanish-inspired dishes:
Black Bean and Feta Quesadilla, 45
Crab Empanadas, 27
Gazpacho, Tropical, 67
Paella Pacifica, 122–23
Spice Island Swordfish Skewers, 128
Spices, 137–38
Spinach:
Baked Eggs with, in Crumb Crust, 56–57
Brunch Torte, 54–55
Lime Soufflé, Salmon in Filo with, 120–21
Parmesan Filo Pizza with, 106
and Shiitake Mushroom Salad, 86
Spring Rolls, Banana, 206–7
Squash:
Butternut, Curried Ragout of Chicken with,
    154
Pumpkin Fritters, Spiced, 58
Vine Leaves Stuffed with Hummus,
    Tabbouleh and, 44
Zucchini Fritters, 60
Star fruit (carambola):
and Chocolate Dessert, 214
Haupia with Banana and, 220
Tropical Fruit Salsa, 190
Stir-fries:
Bok Choy, 164
Chicken, Spicy Lemon-Ginger, 141
Scallop and Shrimp, 124
Stuffing, couscous-nut, 146
Sushi, 28–35
Ahi, Jícama, and Ginger Maki,
    34
Ahi and Jalapeño Maki, 33
Dipping Sauce, 29
rolling, 30
Shrimp, Jícama, and Cilantro Maki, 31
Shrimp and Avocado Maki, 35
Soba and Vegetable Maki, 32
Soba Noodles, 29
Vinegar Rice, 28

Sweet-and-Hot Tropical Fruit Salad, 219
Sweet potato:
    Fritters with Goat Cheese, 61
    Galette, Hawaiian, 109
    and Pear Bisque, 73
Swordfish, 116, *118*
    Seared Marinated, 135
    Skewers, Spice Island, 128

Tabbouleh, 44
    Vine Leaves Stuffed with Squash, Hummus
        and, 44
Tahini, 231
    Hummus, 198
    Lemon Dressing, 99
Tamari, 231
Tamarind:
    paste, 231–32
    Sauce, Hot, Grilled Fish in, 132
Tangerine:
    Sauce, Mahimahi in, 130
    Sauce, Roast Duck in, 146–47
Tapioca with Tropical Fruit, 218
Taro, 232, *232*
Tartlet(s):
    Chicken Salad, Pacific, 46
    Shells, 47
    Shells, Corn, 168
Tarts:
    Banana Tarte Tatin, 212–13
    Macadamia-Lime Mile-High Meringue,
        216–17
Tea, Pacific Plantation, 21
Tequila:
    Margarita, 15
    Margarita Elena, 16
Thai and Thai-inspired dishes:
    Chicken Satay, 149
    Chicken Satay Pizza, 103
    Evil Jungle Prince, 162
    Opal-Basil Coconut Soup, 69
    Paradise Salad, Pacific, 83
Thais, 7, 10, 203
Thyme-Lemon Dressing, 95
Ti leaf, 232, *232*
Tofu, 232
    Cakes, 165
    Oil-Free Miso Dressing, 97
    Pineapple, and Jícama Salad, 84
    Soyannaise, 98

Udon with Vegetables and Gado-Gado
    Sauce, 176
Tomatillos:
    Mexican Fettuccine with Avocado and, 178
    roasting, 187
Tomato(es):
    Basil Filo Pizza, 107
    Cherry, Stuffed with Salmon, 40
    Eggplant, and Chickpea Salad,
        89
    Gazpacho, Tropical, 67
    Ginger Salsa, 191
    roasting, 187
    Stuffed with Goat Cheese, 43
    Sun-Dried-, Sauce, Baked Eggplant with,
        169
    Sun-Dried-, Sauce, Chicken in, 145
Torte, Brunch, 54–55
Tropical fruit:
    Galette with Macadamia-Nut Paste, 221
    Salad, Sweet-and-Hot, 219
    Salsa, 190
    —Stuffed Vine Leaves, 38
    Tapioca and, 218
Tuna. *See* Ahi
Turkey, smoked:
    Brunch Torte, 54–55
    Citrus Muffins with Guava Jelly and, 52

Udon noodles, 232
    cooking, 173
    with Vegetables and Gado-Gado Sauce, 176
    with Wild Mushrooms, 175
Uku, 116, *118*
Ulussoise, 72
Umeboshi, 232
Umu, 8

Vegetable(s):
    Sautéed, Soba with, 174
    and Soba Maki, 32
    Soup with Cilantro Pesto, 70–71
    Udon with, and Gado-Gado Sauce, 176
    see also specific vegetables
Vegetable entrées, 156–69
    Bok Choy Stir-Fry, 164
    Eggplant, Baked, with Sun-Dried-Tomato
        Sauce, 169
    Eggplant in Cinnamon-Chili Sauce, 166
    Evil Jungle Prince, 162

Poblano Peppers, Stuffed, with Mole, 160
Posole, 159
Ratatouille, Oriental, 167
Rosemary Scallop Potato Pie, 163
Tofu Cakes, 165
Vietnamese, 7, 10
Vinegar:
    rice (ingredient), 231
    Rice (for sushi), 28
Vine leaves:
    Stuffed with Squash, Hummus, and
        Tabbouleh, 44
    Tropical Fruit—Stuffed, 38
Volcanoes, Baked, 222–24

Wahoo. *See* Ono
Wasabi, 233
Watercress:
    Paradise Salad, Pacific, 83
    Pasta with Smoked Salmon and, 181
Wine, sparkling, in Pacific Sangría, 18
Wonton wrappers, 233

Yellowtail, *118*
Yogurt-Cucumber Sauce, 199

Zucchini:
    Fritters, 60
    Ratatouille, Oriental, 167
    Soba with Sautéed Vegetables, 174
    Vegetable Soup with Cilantro Pesto, 70–71